George J. Seidel, O.S.B.
St. Martin's College

A Contemporary Approach to Classical Metaphysics

APPLETON-CENTURY-CROFTS
EDUCATIONAL DIVISION
New York MEREDITH CORPORATION

/10
Se4c
92302
Feb. 1975

Preface

This is a textbook for an undergraduate course in metaphysics. It is centered around what have traditionally come to be called the transcendentals, namely being, one, true, good and beauty. It is constructed with as few technical terms as possible; and the two that are used (namely, essence and transcendental) are defined and used in as precise a manner as the tradition will allow. It seems more important to introduce the student into metaphysics itself, rather than simply into one of its terminologies, more or less technical, or its history. Hence, neither does the text provide an overall view of the history of metaphysics. It seems better not to confuse the student with a wealth of historical detail, which can really be appreciated only when the basic notions have first been grasped. Works such as A. O. Lovejoy's *Great Chain of Being* or Etienne Gilson's *Being and Some Philosophers* may be most profitably consulted on this score. However, an initial reading and detailed study of the poem by Parmenides, the father of Western metaphysics, would be most helpful, if not indispensable. For this purpose the main fragments of Parmenides' poem have been included in Appendix I, along with a running commentary and annotated bibliography. For the inclusion of these fragments of Parmenides' poem I wish to express my gratitude to Richmond Lattimore, the translator, and to Appleton-Century-Crofts, who published this translation in M. C. Nahm's *Selections From Early Greek Philosophy* (4 ed., New York, 1962). I have changed the order of some of the fragments to accord with my approach, and have renumbered them in accordance with the ninth edition of Diels' *Fragmente der Vorsokratiker*.

This metaphysics text is called "classical." To some it may appear about as classical as the motorcar, or as Prokofieff's "Classical Symphony," that is, as a modern parody of a classical metaphysics. However, Prokofieff's symphony does use a classic form, and we may speak of even the latest automobile as constructed along "classic lines." For this reason it was thought best to add the words "contemporary approach" to the title. The text is classical in that it derives from, and is based upon, the classics of metaphysical literature; and thus is it able to provide the student with a way back to those classics, so that they may be read with understanding and profit. On the other hand, the text is written with an awareness both of the attacks upon, and of the contributions to, metaphysics as made by modern and contemporary philosophers. These have either been incorporated or parried, as the case might be.

Not everything that could be treated in a course on metaphysics has been included. For example, nothing from the area of what is called "special metaphysics," concerned thematically with God (theodicy), soul (rational psychology) or world (cosmology), has been included. Similarly, there is no treatment of such traditional topics as substance and accident, act and potency, causality, or analogy. The inclusion of such matters tends to introduce long and involved conceptual histories which would take too long to resolve, if they could, indeed, be resolved at the level of an undergraduate textbook. For this reason a list of modern and ancient classics in metaphysics is appended (cf. Appendix II), particularly as available in inexpensive paperback editions, to provide the student with opportunities for further study or correlative outside reading. By the same token, the order of the various topics presented is not to be considered the only one, much less the ideal one. The order in which the various matters are treated often depends upon the questions of the students and the matters they consider next in importance.

The approach has been kept as neutral as possible from presuppositions, certainly from any religious or theological presuppositions. This does not mean that metaphysics is or can be absolutely presuppositionless. One must, for example, be convinced that there are things (other than simply mind or states of mind) that do exist. This is why specific existing beings, for example, the school mascot Ranger, or Felix, the black cat that lives under the old infirmary, are most often used as metaphysical "examples." One might have chosen "the college or university president" as the primary metaphysical example, since he is also normally found on academic campuses. However, this choice might be misinterpreted by the administration; and in any case the latter example is more complicated metaphysically. All that is required to start the course is something that is admitted to exist, other than simply the mind. One can, of course, take the solipsist's position, that there is only one's own mind and its states; but then a course in metaphysics in the classical or traditional sense is out of the question. There is no known cure for the philosophical hypochondria of solipsism, except, perhaps, silence; in which case, naturally, philosophical discourse is ruled out. Similarly, the religious view that the being of God and the world are somehow identical, a position which can be found exemplified in Western as well as in Eastern thought, is, like that of the solipsist, a possible one. However, if one takes this view, it tends to make the intellectual effort involved in understanding the following pages both unnecessary and meaningless.

Finally, a brief but important note on terminology. The terms "thing" and "a being" are used interchangeably, as are the plural words "things" and beings." Likewise, no distinction is made between "being" and "existence." They are to be understood as synonyms. Certain linguistic proprieties do sometimes require that one be used rather than another. It is true that certain contemporary philosophers, for example, Marcel, Heidegger, and Sartre, make a distinction between "being" and "existence." However, it is made within the context of a problematic introduced into contemporary thought by Kierkegaard, and one which does not appear relevant to a course in general, introductory, or classical metaphysics, even though it might be highly relevant to any study of the philosophy of man or what is sometimes called philosophical anthropology.

There are bibliographies at the end of the major sections. The books and articles included do not necessarily represent or support the position taken by the author on the various questions treated. In the different light they throw on that material, however, the reasons for the position the author has taken may be clearer. The periodical most commonly quoted is the *Review of Metaphysics,* since it should be most readily available in college libraries. There are also a series of exercises at the end of the various sections to focus attention on the more important points treated. These can be used by way of review or as material for quizzes.

This work is dedicated to the memory of Monsignor Gerald B. Phelan, late professor of the Mediaeval Institute in Toronto, who is its inspiration; and to my students in metaphysics for the past six years, who have provided much of its material, sharpened the focus of its treatment, and assured me, with the freshness and frankness of youth, that it is the only decent course I teach.

G. J. S.

Contents

Preface   v

I. INTRODUCTION   3

1. Terminology   5
   First Philosophy—Metaphysics—Ontology—Summary
2. The Area of Study   9
3. Question and Answer   11
   Who Is Being?—Why Is Being?—Where Is Being?—How
   Is Being?—When Is Being?—What Is Being?
4. A Being and Being   17
5. Being and Concept   18
6. How Is Being Known?   21
7. Useful and Useless Knowledge   24
8. Summary   28
   Exercises—Bibliography

II. BEING   35

1. Being as Transcendental   37
2. Being as Unlimited   39
3. Essence as Limit   40
4. Aspects of Essence   42

5. Laws of Essence and Existence   45
Do Essences Exist?—Essence and the Parallel of Blind-
ness—Does Being Exist?

6. Does Being Have Anything to Do With Time?   53
7. Summary   59
Exercises—Bibliography

III. THE TRANSCENDENTALS   65

1. One   67
One as Unit—One as Unity—A Being Is One—Does One-
ness Add to Being?—The Determination of Oneness—Individuality and Individuation—Summary—Bibliography

2. True   77
The True and the Real—The Truth of Statements—The
Fact of Error—Truth as Relation: the relation of mind to
thing; the relation of thing to mind—Does Truth Add to
Being?—The Existence of Ideas—Education and Learn-
ing—Summary—Exercises—Bibliography

3. Good   96
Good as Desired—Good as Desirable—The Good and the
True—The Pragmatically Useful and the Good—Summary
—Bibliography

4. Beauty   103
Beauty and the Good—Beauty and Truth—Nature and
Art—Being as Beautiful—Summary—Exercises—Biblio-
graphy

APPENDIX I. Parmenides and His Poem   112
The Prologue—The Way of Truth—The Way of Seeing
—The Significance of Parmenides—Bibliography

APPENDIX II. Suggested Paperback Material for Historical   122
Background

Index   125

I
INTRODUCTION

This rather lengthy introductory part, approximately a third of the text, is devoted to fixing the area and object of study. One problem is the very title and the meaning to be attached to the traditional titles for the course. These are discussed briefly in the very first section, as also the influence which the scientific world-view can have upon the matter of our study. But even more difficult is the material itself, and how it is to be approached. What is the right question to ask regarding our subject matter in order to obtain a meaningful answer? For if we would ask the wrong question, we might be off the track from the start. Perhaps, there is no way to determine the right question. Metaphysics may be one of these places whose location we cannot get to from here. Hence the third section is devoted to the various questions which have been asked or could be asked about being. After clarifying one of these questions in the tradition, we will proceed, by way of a metaphysical example, to the way in which being would be known, the relation of being to concept, to what is sensed, concluding that being is simply included or presupposed in all knowing. Finally, the question of the speculative and the practical in relation to metaphysics is considered: whether metaphysics, or any knowledge for that matter, can be considered purely speculative. And toward the end of this final section there is a brief review of useless and impractical studies, their meaning and possible motivation.

1. TERMINOLOGY

a. First Philosophy

The area of study which we are here considering has passed itself under a variety of aliases. The use of one or the other name, in order to designate or characterize the subject matter of the course, has often indicated and specified the approach taken. Thus, what we are studying has been called the Science of First Principles or First Philosophy, since it was understood as the most basic of philosophical disciplines, and that upon which all the other parts of philosophy would necessarily depend. Aristotle gave this name of First Philosophy (*protē philosophia*) to the study of the principles, first causes, and essential attributes of being as being, more specifically, to the study of that separate and unchangeable being to which he gave the term "theology." This is obviously not theology as it developed in the West after the introduction of Christianity, which study depends primarily upon the basic data of a revelation believed to be from God, but rather the attempt on the part of human reason to go as far as it could in its attempts to understand what truly exists and the ultimate causes and reasons for what does thus exist.

b. Metaphysics

Another word used to describe our subject matter is the word Metaphysics. If the word was not actually used by Aristotle, it was, nevertheless, used to designate that section of the body of Aristotle's works which come "after" (*meta*) the physics (*ta physica.*)[1] There is, however, an ambiguity in the *meta* of meta-physics. The Greek preposition can mean "after," as that which in the arrangement of Aristotle's works was placed after the *Physics*. However, the preposition can also have the meaning of "above" or "beyond," in the sense that metaphysics is concerned with that which lies above and beyond the physical. The designation "metaphysics" is not, then, simply an editorial convenience in order to classify a certain body of material in the Aristotelian *corpus;* it is also, to some extent, an accurate characterization of what is therein considered, namely that which is over and above the physical.

It must be borne in mind, however, that the word "physics" had a very different meaning for the Greeks than it has for us. The Greek word *physis* was translated into the Latin *natura,* and thus, eventually, into our English word "nature."[2] From this one might be led to believe that metaphysics studies what is above and beyond nature; hence, it is concerned with "super-nature" or with the "supernatural." But although Aristotle did, in fact, use the word theology to designate more specifically the matter of this area of study, metaphysics is not theology in our sense of that word, nor is it one of the occult sciences.

In order to understand the meaning of physics in the Greek sense, and thus also that which is "beyond the physics," it is necessary to recall the root of the Greek word, which, like its Latin translation into *natura,* derives, or is at least related to, the word meaning "to grow" and "to develop" (*phyo*). For the Greeks conceived nature, the cosmos as a whole, as something fundamentally alive. It had a soul, because, like anything alive, it was self-moving. The Greeks made no sharp distinction between the organic and the inorganic. The world as a whole was seen as something alive, a view very different from the dead and lifeless universe envisioned by Descartes in the seventeenth century, who saw the physical universe solely in

---

[1] A.–H. Chroust, "Origin of the Word Metaphysics," *Review of Metaphysics,* 14 (1961) 601–616; Hans Reiner, "Die Enstehung der Lehre von Bibliothekarischen Ursprung des Namens Metaphysik," *Zeitschrift für philosophische Forschung,* 9 (1955) 77–99.

[2] For a review of the sixty-six different meanings of "Nature" in Western thought, see: A. O. Lovejoy and George Boas, *Primitivism and Related Ideas in Antiquity* (Baltimore: Johns Hopkins, 1935), Appendix: "Some Meanings of 'Nature'," pp. 447–456.

terms of matter (which was essentially extension) and motion.[3]

Indeed, Aristotle considered the physical world under the aspect of motion or mobile being. However, the ultimate cause or causes of that motion were within the cosmos itself, in the unmoved mover (or movers) on the outer fringe of the cosmos. For this reason there was also a basic teleology, or purposefulness, to all the motions and changes which took place in the sublunary world, since all causality, including therefore final causality, would derive from forces within the cosmos itself.[4] In Descartes, on the other hand, the initial cause of all the motion in the universe was to be imputed to a First Cause outside the extended world of matter and motion; and there could be no inquiry into the final causes, which could only lie in the mind and in the inscrutable designs of the First Cause.[5] One might characterize the difference between the physical world of Aristotle and that of Descartes as the difference between an organism and a machine. For the Greek to conceive of the cosmos solely in terms of extension and motion, as little more than a machine, would have seemed contrary to experience. The Greek experienced his world in terms of its recurring seasons, spring giving way to summer, the death of winter passing into the rebirth of spring. Similar periodic, self-sustaining motions could be found in the movements of the heavenly bodies as well. All things operated in living and harmonious fashion in terms of causes and reasons within the cosmos itself.

The fundamentally different way in which the world of physics would be viewed by the Greek and by the Cartesian would also have its effect upon the view that one took of metaphysics, as that which is over and above the physics. This is no less true of the present-day view of the physical world which we accept from the natural sciences or through modern physics. This does not, of course, mean that it is necessary to return to the Greek view of the world in order to do metaphysics; but it does mean that we must be aware of the fact and of the way in which certain presuppositions from a view of nature, which is more or less scientific, the view one takes of physics, can color the approach taken toward that which is over and above the "physics."

[3] R. G. Collingwood, *The Idea of Nature* (New York: Galaxy Books, 1960), pp. 29–92.
[4] See Aristotle, *Physics* II, 1; *Metaphysics* V, 4.
[5] See Descartes, *Principles of Philosophy*, I, 26–28; II, 4–22.

c.   Ontology

Another term used to describe the matter of our study is the word *ontology*.[6] Since the word is made up of two Greek words, *logos* (study or science) and *ontos* (the participial form of the Greek verb "to be"), one might be led to believe that the application of this term for the study of being would be of Greek origin. Certainly the science or study of being is of Greek origin, and the etymology of the term is also Greek, but the term ontology derives more immediately from Christian Wolff, the eighteenth century follower and systematizer of the philosophy of Gottfried Leibniz. Hence, it should come as no surprise that the ontology of a philosopher and mathematician, such as Leibniz or Wolff, both of them after Descartes and affected by the physical and mathematical view of the physical world introduced by the new physics, should be radically different from the meta-physics of Aristotle and those mediaeval thinkers who tended to follow him. The general and special ontology of a Wolff could not but be colored by this fact. This may also succeed in throwing some light upon the rejection of ontology, and this particular way of doing metaphysics, by Immanuel Kant in the latter part of the eighteenth century.

d.   Summary

From this it may readily be seen that there are different kinds of metaphysics. Metaphysics does not represent a large body of generally agreed upon knowledge, as does chemistry or biology, for example. There are different ways of doing metaphysics. This would be so if only because the view one takes of the physical universe would have an important bearing upon the way in which the "metaphysical" might be viewed. Metaphysics is not something done in an airtight, hermetically sealed ivory tower, as though there were no external influences upon the way in which a man thinks about matters at their most fundamental level. For example, a philosopher must make use of a language. And as Wittgenstein rightly pointed out, the very language that the philosopher must use can bewitch his thought. External influences from the society within which one lives, or from the scientific world view prevalent in the period, all these

---

[6]J.–F. Mora, "On the Early History of 'Ontology'," *Philosophy and Phenomenological Research*, 24 (1963) 36–47.

can have a bearing on the way metaphysics will be done. This can be seen in the works of Aristotle himself. It may have been later editors who were responsible for the division of the body of Aristotle's works into physics and metaphysics; however, in Aristotle's *Physics* there is a great deal of metaphysics, and in Aristotle's *Metaphysics* there is a great deal of what even he understands as physics.

2. THE AREA OF STUDY

Metaphysics studies being. This is clearly a rather large area of study. For if everything that exists is to be included within the compass of treatment—and there would be no way of excluding it—then the philosophy of being would end up studying absolutely everything. Thus, unless some specific approach to everything that exists could be established at the start, the task of metaphysics would become impossibly large and hopelessly vague. And how would metaphysics, then, be differentiated from the many other sciences that deal with the things that exist?[7] For does not every science study being in some way, shape, or form? After all, nuclear physics is concerned with being, namely the being of the atom and the subatomic. Biology is also concerned with being, that is, with living being. Sociology is interested in what exists, namely with the existence of human societies, their structures and the functions of members within them. One might say that all these sciences study being from their own respective and specific points of view—being as subatomic, as living, as social—but that metaphysics studies being from no particular aspect or point of view. Metaphysics simply studies straight, ungarnished being. But this tends to leave the task of the metaphysician in the same hopeless vagueness with which it began, studying everything, from no particular aspect or point of view,

[7]On the question of the division and classification of the sciences, see Thomas Aquinas, *The Division and Methods of the Sciences*, tr. A. Maurer. 2 ed. (Toronto: Institute of Mediaeval Studies, 1958); Robert McRae, *The Problem of the Unity of the Sciences: Bacon to Kant* (Toronto: Toronto University Press, 1961.)

simply because of the obvious truism that everything that exists does, in fact, exist.

One might, of course, find something comparable to the problem of studying being in the task of studying man. It might be pointed out that psychology studies man, as does sociology, cultural anthropology, history, physiology, etc.; but that it is possible to distinguish each of these sciences from the others by the slightly different point of view that each takes in relation to their common study of man. Thus we say that psychology studies man in terms of his behaviour patterns; or that sociology studies man in his interrelationships with his fellow human beings and in terms of the institutions that he forms. Or we say that history studies man in terms of his past, as cultural anthropolgy studies man in terms of the "cultural leftovers" that perdure from a distant prehistorical past. Clearly each one of these sciences, as also the physiology which considers man as a physical organism, studies man, but each from a specific point of view.

Or one might take a slightly different example. There are different ways of looking at a tree. For the botanist a tree is a genus and species of living things; and thus is he able to study and classify trees. For the "tree doctor," on the other hand, a tree is either sick or healthy, requiring this or that mineral or fertilizer to make or keep it healthy. For the landscape architect a tree is something to be set in a certain place for its shade or beauty. For the poet or the painter the tree may provide the inspiration for a poem or be the model for a painting; it is a thing to be admired for its beauty and its grace. For the lumberjack, however, the tree is something to be felled in a certain direction, and sent to the mill. For the mill owner the tree is so many board feet.

There are many ways of looking at a tree, just as there are many different points of view that one can take regarding man. One cannot take all possible views simultaneously. Neither can any one science hope to deal with absolutely everything. Hence, to say that because everything that exists is the concern of the philosophy of being in that it exists, we are left with a subject even broader than that of man. It is, of course, true that metaphysics can use anything that exists as an example for its consideration of being; however, this can be done only after the area and approach of our subject has been more carefully specified and delineated.

A slightly different approach for localizing the area of our study may be taken from a more recent philosopher. Martin Heidegger writes in his brief work "What is Metaphysics?": "Science does not want to know anything about nothing."[8] For example, the physicist is interested in physical reality and *nothing* else; the biologist, in living organisms and *nothing* else; the economist, in gross national products and *nothing* else, etc. What Heidegger suggests is that the metaphysician is the one interested in these "nothings," namely that which none of the other various special sciences are interested in. In this way the metaphysician need not worry about trespassing on grounds already occupied by the special sciences: what they are interested in, he is not; what he is interested in, they are not. They do not want to know anything about nothing, that is, about being. The metaphysician, it would appear, studies what is left after all the various special sciences have picked over everything else. There is certainly a great deal of value in looking at the matter in this light, although it does not bring out sufficiently well the fundamentally basic character of that which metaphysics studies. After all, the special sciences would have literally nothing at all to study were it not for the existence of that nothing which they are not really interested in studying.

3. QUESTION AND ANSWER

The approaches used above do not seem to have clarified sufficiently well the subject of our study. In fact, we may be using the wrong approach entirely, asking the wrong sort of question from the start. In his dialogue the *Meno* Plato puts the following words into the mouth of Meno regarding the whole problem of asking questions:

You argue that a man cannot enquire either about that which he knows, or about that which he does not know; for if he knows, he has no need to

[8]Martin Heidegger, "What Is Metaphysics?" *Existence and Being*, ed. W. Brock (Chicago: Regnery Gateway, 1949), pp. 328–329; see also Heidegger, *The Question of Being*, trs. W. Kluback and J. T. Wilde (New York: Twayne, 1958), pp. 96ff. Taking a very different view of Heidegger is Rudolf Carnap, "The Elimination of Metaphysics Through Logical Analysis of Language," *Logical Positivism*, ed. A. J. Ayer (Glencoe, N. Y.: Free Press, 1959).

enquire; and if not, he cannot; for he does not know the very subject about which he is to enquire. (80e, Jowett tr.)

What Plato suggests is that in order to ask the right question, we must already know the answer. But if the enquirer knows the answer, then why ask the question; and if he does not know the answer, how can he ask, since he does not know even in what direction to begin the enquiry? For if he did not know the answer before asking the question, he might actually have the answer in his hand, but fail to recognize it, because he would have no idea what the answer might look like. Plato's "answer" to this question in the dialogue was, of course, his theory of recollection, namely that the mind already possesses the "answers" to the sensible objects it meets in experience through the ideas attached to the soul, contemplated by the soul before it was lodged in a body.

Although one may have legitimate philosophical doubts about Plato's theory of recollection, particularly with the theory of the pre-existence of the soul contemplating the ideas in the Platonic heaven before birth, which the doctrine seems to require, there is a great deal of truth to what Plato says about the relation between question and answer. Clearly, we need not know the whole answer in order to be able to ask a question, otherwise, indeed, there would be no need to ask the question in the first place, as Plato indicates; still, we may be required to have some inkling of the answer. Even more pertinent to our present problem, however, is the suggestion that it is possible to ask the wrong question at the start. It is possible to ask a question for which there is no answer ("How high is up?") or one whose answer is prejudiced by the question itself ("When did you stop beating your wife?"). Asking the right question is of particular importance in metaphysics. And the various ways in which the question of being might be posed interrogatively are worthy of consideration, no matter how odd the questions may at first sight appear.

a.   Who Is Being?

For example, if we ask the question, "Who is being?" we sense immediately that we are asking the wrong question. Not only is the question grammatically suspicious, but the answer expected would have to be personal. The question would hardly be worth our consideration if its answer had not actually been given by philosophers in the past. The answer to the question "Who is being?" could be given by solipsism; which might be interpreted as saying, "I exist, but I'm not so sure about you, or anything else for that matter, unless you or those other things exist as my states of mind." Similarly, in answer to the question, "Who is being?", one might say "God is being," since God would be a person, in fact, in such a case, perhaps the only person. But this would mean that being or the existence of everything that exists must be somehow identical with God, which would appear to be some sort of pantheism. Indeed, the identification of God with the world is a possible intellectual option, as is solipsism; however, there are certain difficulties in posing and answering the question in this way.

The basic difficulty in giving a "personal" answer to the question of being is that it requires us to posit a consciousness (and some sort of will) to everything that exists, no matter how primitive the level of consciousness or elementary the grade of willing may be. We may, indeed, be willing to grant to animals a level of consciousness and will. But do we wish to consider the tropism of the sunflower constantly turning toward the sun as a result of consciousness or freedom? Do rocks and lakes have consciousness? Clearly to use the word consciousness, particularly in these latter two senses would appear to milk it of anything like the ordinary meaning that it has when applied to conscious beings such as men. The question "Who is being?" is the wrong question.

b.　Why Is Being?

One might pose the question of being in the form, "Why is being?" A similar question has, in fact, been posed in the history of Western thought. Leibniz, for example, asked "Why is there something rather than nothing?" Or Friedrich Schelling asked, "Why is there not nothing? Why is there anything at all?" Clearly this is a very different sort of question than "Who is being?", and one that appears to make the bottom fall out of everything we experience as real and true. Nevertheless, the question would appear to be a theological one, rather than one for philosophy; for the answer would seem to be a creator God, who is then understood, for example in

Leibniz, as the sufficient or grounding reason why there is something rather than nothing, since he would be the ultimate cause thereof. But aside from the fact that the question does not seem to be a philosophical one, there is another basic difficulty: it runs counter to the facts. It is a hypothetical, rather than a real question. There *is* something rather than absolutely nothing. This is the main, if not the only, basic presupposition for the course. The question implies a condition contrary to the fact; and then attempts to pose a question concerning this hypothetical situation. The question "Why is being?" cannot be the right metaphysical question.

c. Where Is Being?

The possible answers to the question "Where is being?" are many. One can say that being is here; it is there; it is everywhere. This would seem to leave being all over the place, thus making its localized study impossible. Further, besides saying that being is here, there, and everywhere, we could also say that it is "nowhere." It does not have a particular "where" in space in the same way that this table or that dog has a specific where. The "where" of being would be like the "nothing" that the special sciences are simply not interested in studying, since it is not something that can be specified and localized in some scientific fashion. In other words, the question "Where is being?" points to everywhere and to nowhere. As such it would represent only a vague and useless answer to our question.

d. How Is Being?

The question "How is being?" suffers from grammatical defects which would render it meaningless. Thus in answer to the question "How is being?" one might answer, "It's fine. How are you?" Normally, however, a "how" question is a scientific question: "How does a particular compound react to such and such a chemical?" But if we attempt to ask the same sort of question of being, namely "How does being work?", the answer would be, "That depends upon what kind of being we are talking about; they work in different ways." A physical organism does not work in the same way that an inanimate object does; and a scientific, rather than a metaphysical, description of how they do work would be better suited to the question of "how being is." There is, as we shall see, a sense in which the question "How is being?" can be a genuinely metaphysical question. Thus the answer to the question "How does being exist?" will be able to throw a very important light upon the meaning of being. But before the answer to that question can be attempted, a great many other points must be settled.

e.   When Is Being?

One might, of course, ask "When is being?" This introduces the element of time into our consideration of being. There is no difficulty in answering simply "now." What exists at present is what exists. But then what of the past and the future? What did exist and what will exist do not, by definition, exist at present, otherwise we would not use the past and future tenses of the verb "to be" in speaking about what no longer exists or what does not yet exist. In a sense, however, not even the "now" of what is at present exists; since what was now is no longer now, and what will soon be now is not yet now. Then too, one might argue that the past and the future also have something to do with being, in that the past was "in being," and the future, barring unforeseen circumstances, will be "in being." Clearly, the question "When is being?" and the whole relation of being and time is highly complex, and could not operate as the most basic question we might ask about being. In any case it could not be approached in any adequate fashion until a whole host of other questions had been answered. Indeed, the question will occupy an important place at the end of part II.

f.   What Is Being?

At first sight the most obvious question that might be asked in relation to being would seem to be the simple interrogative "What is being?" Such was the question that Aristotle asked of being: *ti to on?* Indeed, when we want to know what something is, this is the question that we ask. In relation to being, however, the question labors under certain difficulties. For example, we may ask the question "What is a dog?" and give a definition which will cover every animal that is mammal, vertebrate, canine, domesticated, etc. In thus defining dog as a specific sort of animal, however, we make use of what is non-dog; for there are also things which are not dogs, namely all those animals which are invertebrate, undomesticated, etc., as well as the innumerable non-dog things that are not animals. Thus we have a class of animals carefully and logically circumscribed; everything that is a dog falls into the class, and the class is circumscribed by everything that is non-dog.

non-dog   (dog)

If, however, we attempt to define being as the class of all things that exist, we immediately run into a problem. In the case of dog we could use what is non-dog in order to establish the class. But what might be used to define or delineate the class of being, that is, of all things that exist? For there is no non-being which might possibly be used to define being as a class, since, by definition, non-being does not exist. There is, then, literally nothing that might be used actually to constitute the "class" of being.

non-being   (being)

But if it is impossible to define being in this way, then the question "What is being?", taken in this sense, cannot be the right question. Whatever being is, it is not something that can be given a definition in the way that dog and cat, as the classes of canine and feline domesticated mammals respectively, are given a definition. Being cannot be understood as a logical class of all classes, for there is literally nothing that could be used to define such a class except non-being, which, by definition, does not exist.

One might even say that there are psychological hazards in treating being or that which is as a class. One can, for example, attempt to discover "happiness" in this way. One merely divides all things and people into two classes, those things and people that "exist," and those which "do not exist." One then makes the class of those things that "exist" very small and restrictive, and the things and people e.g., professors) that "do not exist" very large, and ignores the latter class, because it does not exist. The trouble with such a class approach to things that exist is that, unfortunately, the class of things and people that "do not exist" can be very bothersome at times. The psychological hazard would be that of schizophrenia, with the possibility of a complication of paranoia.

More seriously, however, there is a certain ambiguity in the question "What is being?" which may be of some assistance in propelling forward our consideration of the way in which to approach being. In Aristotle the question can be interpreted as meaning either "What is being as being?" or "What is *a* being?" (in the sense of any particular, individual thing). Clearly, if we take the question to refer to being as being, in the sense of the class of all beings, because of the fact that all beings have being in common, then the question is certainly the wrong one. But if we take the question "What is being?" in the sense "What is a particular being?" a different road is opened up for our inquiry.

4. A BEING AND BEING

In order to ask the question in this different sense we might take the example of a specific being, namely the school mascot, Ranger. Since Ranger is a being, we might simply substitute for the question "What is a being?" the question "What is Ranger?" And the answer is simply: he is a white Samoyede. The zoologist might go further and define him as a domesticated mammal, vertebrate, canine, etc. One might note various other qualities and characteristics possessed by Ranger, namely that he is a male, cowardly, and stupid. However, in all the careful listing that one might make of the various qualities and characteristics possessed by this particular white Samoyede, whether of a scientific or of a purely descriptive nature, there is one "quality" which is most often forgotten and very easily ignored, namely the fact that Ranger *exists*.

One might, of course, say that the fact of Ranger's existence is simply assumed or taken for granted when we say that "Ranger *is* a white Samoyede." This may, indeed, be true; but it is not necessarily the case. For we may say "Cerberus is a big, black watchdog," which does not *necessarily* imply that the quality or characteristic of existence is possessed by Cerberus, the mythological watchdog guarding the gates of the nether world. Thus we can say, "A triangle *is* a three-sided figure" or, "A leprechaun *is* an Irish dwarf," when there are no such things as perfectly three-sided figures, and when we may have serious doubts about the existence of leprechauns. In other words, although it is true that Ranger, the school mascot, exists, our use of the word "is" in a proposition describing something about Ranger does not necessarily imply existence. The various forms of the verb "to be" can be used grammatically in a purely copulative function, that is, as merely joining together two ideas or concepts in the mind, which concepts or ideas may, or may not, have any existence independently of the mind's thinking them. It is, of course, the business of logic to analyse the logical relations between propositions of one sort or another, what they imply or entail. However, we are not concerned here with logic, but with metaphysics. Our interest is not in the logical demarcation of classes and subclasses of things or in the logical form or format of propositions, or even, primarily, in what may, or may not, be said about Ranger, whether from a logical or purely empirical point of view, but with the fact that Ranger *exists,* and with the meaning of this fact. Indeed, if Ranger did not, in fact, exist, all those things we might say about him, the various qualities or characteristics that might be ascribed to such an "idea," as in the case of Cerberus above, would have a very different sense. However, the kind of existence that an idea or a concept would possess will have to await treatment until we come to the question of truth and its relation to being. Still, at this point it can be seen that existence would be a very peculiar "quality," if only because it is the most fundamental one. For if the "a being" did not have the "quality" of existence, it would have none of the qualities which it actually has. This particular quality would represent an absolutely necessary condition for all the other qualities which would actually be said of any "a being."

5.   BEING AND CONCEPT

Kant denied that being can be a quality in any sense. Thus in his *Critique of Pure Reason* he writes:

'Being' is obviously not a real predicate; that is, it is not a concept of
something which could be added to the concept of a thing. . . . A hundred
real thalers do not contain the least coin more than a hundred possible
thalers. (A 598–9, B 626–7).

What Kant says is, of course, entirely true. The concept of existence
will add nothing to the concept we have of a thing. There is no difference between the concept of a hundred real and a hundred
possible thalers. Kant does not, of course, deny that there may be a
great deal of difference between an actual hundred real thalers in
my purse and the hundred possible thalers which I may receive
tomorrow in payment of a debt. The one is in my purse; the other
may never be there. This is not what he means by "possible." His
point is, rather, that so far as the conceptual content of the two are
concerned the hundred real and the hundred possible thalers are the
same.
     The key word in the passage is, however, the word concept. The
concept of existence adds nothing to the concept we have of a thing.
But Kant says something, however indirectly, about existence when
he says this. For perhaps the reason why the concept of existence
would add nothing to the concept we have of something is because
being or existence is not a concept. Indeed, if it were a concept we
might expect it to add something to the conceptual content of another concept. We have not as yet determined exactly what kind of
existence a concept or an idea might have (this question must remain "on the shelf" until we come to the section on truth), but it is
clear even at this stage of the discussion that existence and concept
cannot be equated; and whatever kind of existence a concept would
have, it could not be the same as the existence that a being would
have. The existence of Felix, the cat living under the old infirmary,
is not the existence of a concept; otherwise whoever was thinking of
the existence of Felix might stop thinking that concept, and Felix
would cease to exist. In any case, no cat could chase many mice on a
purely conceptual existence. Felix' existence is something very real;
so much so that if she did not have this particular "quality," she
would, in actual fact, have no other.
     It must, however, be granted that the "quality" of being or exist-
ence is a peculiar sort of quality. In the case of Felix, for example, it

is not a quality like that of black, "good mouser," if only because it is a necessary condition for these qualities. She would not be black, nor would she purr, unless she actually existed. In this sense it is a predicate, though a predicate admittedly different from those other qualities or predicates which may be predicated of Felix.

In his *Science of Logic*, Hegel states that "Pure Being and pure Nothing are, then, the same." Hegel does not say that they are identical, but that they are the same. They are the same, as he explains the matter, in "becoming," since in becoming what is and what is not slip into each other.[9] What Hegel says is entirely true, given the abstract conceptual level at which he is speaking. Pure being is pure immediacy and total indeterminacy (since it could be defined only by non-being), and is thus coterminous with the complete emptiness of nothing. Pure being and pure nothing are the same because there is no way to differentiate them or to define that difference. "Pure" in this context means nonempirical. There is no way in which to differentiate pure being and pure nothing at the level of the abstract; it is not possible to "define" being by non-being, any more than it would be possible to define non-being by being.

From what we have seen above, particularly in connection with the question "What is being?" what Hegel says is entirely true: It is impossible to define being, except by non-being, which would define nothing. But the difficulty which Hegel encounters here may be similar to that of Kant; being is taken as though it were a concept. It may be true that the pure concept of being is the same as the pure concept of non-being—pure indeterminacy may be indistinguishable from complete emptiness—nevertheless, the being or existence of a being is not that of a concept. Much less is the existence of a being the same as non-being, that is, if the "a being" does, in fact, exist. Pure being and pure non-being have no relation whatever to the being or existence of a being. And in order to say that they are the same one must consider the being of a being at a purely abstract level.

As is clear both in Kant and in Hegel, however indirectly this truth may be expressed, being cannot be a concept. As a concept being would have no conceptual content, as Kant rightly saw. And if being is understood at the level of abstract concept or in the manner

[9]G. W. F. Hegel, *Science of Logic*, trs. W. H. Johnston and L. G. Struthers (London: G. Allen, 1959), I, 95–120.

of an abstract logic, then, as it may be seen from Hegel, being is indistinguishable from nothing. Being cannot be defined; it is as indeterminate and empty, when conceived abstractly, as nothing. Metaphysics cannot define being.

This inability on the part of the metaphysician to define being, to give a precise conceptual delineation of the primary matter of his concern, is not, however, a peculiarity of metaphysics. The same is true, in one way or another, with the primary subject of discussion in any science or art. Which artist can say what beauty is? Which jazz musician can define improvisation? Or which physicist can explain exactly what he means by energy? Can the biologist tell us what life is? Does the sociologist ever define what he means by society, except by saying that it is some sort of "group?" And yet these are the central areas of concern around which all their research and intellectual or artistic activity is oriented. In other words, metaphysics is not unique in its inability to define that about which it is most concerned.

6.   HOW IS BEING KNOWN?

The being or existence of a being—and throughout we are concerned with the *being* of a being—is not that of an abstract concept. Nor, as we have seen, can being be known or determined conceptually. From a purely conceptual point of view being or existence is indistinguishable from non-being or nothing. How, then, is being known? Why, for example, in the description of Ranger above, of all the various qualities and characteristics that he possesses, was his existence so easily ignored. Perhaps, one might say, the being or existence of a being gets passed over unobserved because most of our knowing, at least in the West, is conceptual or conceptually grounded, and this is why we fail to advert to the fact of existence or being. But if the being or existence of a being is not known conceptually, then how, in fact, is it known? How is it experienced?

Perhaps, one might say, it is experienced or grasped perceptually. But to perceive is, presumably, to perceive through the senses. And although I may perceive the carrot as orange, fibrous, and tasty, what color, taste, or consistency might the *existence* of the carrot be said to have? Similarly I can perceive the fact that Ranger is white, furry, barking, and has been chasing skunks again; yet it is not possible to say that the existence of Ranger is white, furry, barking, and smelly. We can smell the odor of skunk on Ranger, but we cannot smell his existence. We can pet Ranger, but we cannot say that we pet his existence. We can hear him barking, but we do not hear whatever noise his existence might make. What kind of noise does an existence make? We can see what color the carrot is, but does its existence have a color? We can experience the carrot as sweet to the taste; but what would the existence of the carrot taste like? It would appear that we cannot perceive existence or being; we lack senses appropriate to its perception.

The fact that we do not perceive the being or existence of a being, even though we do in a variety of ways perceive the "a being" itself, may appear as something of an anomaly. However, it is not a wholly peculiar anomaly. Similar curiosities occur as a result of the world-view of the modern physicist or chemist. For example, modern science tells us that glass is not a solid, but a liquid. It merely happens to flow very slowly. Or it will tell us that the reason why the coffee cup holds the coffee is because the holes in the "material" of the coffee cup—which coffee cup, incidentally, is in a constant and vibrating motion—happen to be smaller than the size of the coffee molecules which the cup contains. This is clearly not how we perceive windows and coffee cups, but science would assure us that this is still the way they are.

But if we do not have a percept of the being or existence of a being, any more than we have a concept of it, then how is it known? Some philosophers have suggested that being or existence is known by intuition. By intuition they seem to mean a knowledge—producing experience which is nonconceptual. Unfortunately, the attempt to describe a knowledge which is nonconceptual in terms that are also nonconceptual proves extremely difficult. Furthermore, the meaning of the word is not helped by the tradition. In Descartes, for example, the word intuition is used to describe an intellectual "seeing" of the "clear and distinct ideas." In Kant, on the other hand, intuition (*Anschauung*) is sensible; and the pure intuitions of space and time, the forms of sensibility. If intuition would produce the clear and distinct ideas, it should have the clarity of conceptual knowledge, which, as we have seen in the case of being, would insure that being had not, in fact, been grasped in this way. If being were a sensible intuition or a product of its forms, it should be specifiable in perceptual experience, which, as we have seen, it is not. One could, of course, speak of the intuition of being as a "sympathy with being," as does Henri Bergson, a "feeling" for being, or an "attunement to it." However, the meaning of such terms would be decidely vague until the basis for such a sympathy, feeling, or attuning were made clear. And to say that it is intuition which grasps this meaning, and also provides the basis for its grasping, is to beg the question at its most basic level.

Some recent philosophers have attempted to characterize our knowledge of being as similar to our awareness of presence, contrasting it with the experience of absence. Thus if I go to a café, expecting to meet Pierre, to take J.-P. Sartre's example, and fail to find him, I experience the absence of Pierre.[10] The converse of my experience of absence is that of being or existence as presence. The difficulty with attempting to experience being in this way, as a presence which is the total opposite of absence, is that there is no such experience of total absence. When I go to the café expecting to meet Pierre, and he is not there; there may, indeed, be no Pierre, but there is still a café, with tables and chairs and other people, drinking, smoking, and talking. The experience of total absence is simply not given; for there would be literally nothing that could be given either. For even if Pierre should be present in the café, one might argue that his existence or being could not be totally present there. If it were, he could never be present anywhere else. And even so far as his presence in the café is concerned it is still difficult to know exactly in what way his presence is "given," and thus how the being of that "a being" would be known.

Thomas Aquinas probably gave as good a reason as any for why we ignore or forget being when he said: "For that which first falls under apprehension is being, whose understanding is included in whatever one apprehends." (ST I–II, 94, 2, c.) He suggests that the reason we do not perceive or have a concept of being is because it is included (*includitur*) in everything that we actually know or apprehend, as part and parcel of any perceptual knowledge we might

[10]J.–P. Sartre, *Being and Nothingness,* tr. H. E. Barnes (London: Metheun, 1957), pp. 9ff.

have, and from which any conceptual knowledge would be drawn. Being or existence simply goes unnoticed; but it is necessarily implied, Aquinas asserts, in whatever we know. And this primary apprehension, one may say, provides the basis upon which one may go on to a more reflective consideration of what it means to be, such as is undertaken in metaphysics. One reason, perhaps, why being tends to go unnoticed is because absolutely everything that exists has being; and we fail to advert to something so seemingly commonplace and ordinary, simply because everything has it. It is ordinarily taken for granted, like the noises of the city, for example, are taken for granted by the city dweller. They are simply not adverted to; and are "noticed" only in their absence, that is, in their silence. This is, perhaps, the kernel of truth contained in the views of certain recent philosophers that our knowledge of the meaning of being derives from certain negative phenomena; for example, from the experience of absence, the unmasking of delusion or hallucination, the vague anxiety which is an uneasy fear of "nothing" in particular, etc. This could not, however, imply an integral experience of being, if only because its opposite, absence, can never be experienced in its totality.

.7. USEFUL AND USELESS KNOWLEDGE

Before proceeding much further it might be well to admit what the reader may have already begun to suspect; namely, that the study of metaphysics represents a piece of useless knowledge. According to the philosophical tradition of the West there are essentially two kinds of knowledge, speculative and practical. Speculative knowledge is concerned primarily with interpreting and understanding what actually exists. It has nothing essentially to do with speculation, in the sense that one might speculate in stocks and bonds. Neither does it have anything essentially to do with the conditional or the hypothetical. Speculative knowledge is concerned with understanding and interpreting what is or exists. Practical knowledge, on the other hand, is concerned less with what *is* than with what *is to be.* The practical knowledge which one possesses need not necessarily be put into practice. Thus a professor of agricultural science may not actually be a farmer, or the teacher of engineering, an engineer; and yet their knowledge is eminently practical, in that it can or could be put into practical benefit. It must be granted that there can be many speculative or theoretical elements in the practical knowledge one might possess or impart. In agricultural science, for example, the theory of chemistry is necessarily implied; in engineering, physics and mathematics. But although there can be certain practical applications of theoretical or speculative knowledge, still, the distinction between a knowledge fundamentally ordained toward the practical, and one which is not, remains a valid one.

In his work on truth (*De Veritate I*, 1) Thomas Aquinas also makes this traditional distinction. He says that it is for the wise man to order (*sapientis est ordinare*). This ordering, he says, can take place in two essentially different ways: there is an order which is simply there, and thus an order which can be speculated or theorized about (*ordo speculationis*); or there is an order which is not there, or at least not yet there, but one which man sets about to establish (*ordo stabiliationis*). This latter order, for Aquinas, represents the ordering of "art," taking that word in the broad sense of the Greek word "poetics" (from *poein*, meaning any kind of doing or making). It is also the ordering which man attempts to establish in his life of action; this moral order or ordering is the consideration of another area of philosophy, namely that of ethics.

It should be recognized immediately that the area of philosophy we are studying here is not practical. There is no immediate application of the knowledge provided by metaphysics. It is not a knowledge ordained toward the practical order. Metaphysics represents useless knowledge. Karl Marx in his *Theses on Feuerback*, xi, noted this when he said that, "The philosophers have only *interpreted* the world, in various ways; the point, however, is to *change* it." Implicitly Marx recognized that philosophy is essentially nonpractical, concerned with a theoretical or speculative understanding and interpretation of the world, and thus not primarily concerned with the practical matter of changing it. This is precisely his objection to it.

One might, however, ask to what extent a speculative knowledge, even one so apparently useless as metaphysics, is totally nonpractical? In what sense is it possible to speak of a purely speculative knowledge? And here Marx is himself a case in point. For Marx was himself a metaphysician, or at least derived some of the basic ideas for his philosophy from one of the greatest metaphysicians of modern times, namely Hegel. And one would hardly say that the metaphysical speculations of Marx, or in the final analysis those of Hegel, have not had the most profound influence upon our world. In other words, even the most speculative of knowledge can have practical applications and implications. There does not appear to be any purely speculative, that is, totally useless knowledge; any more than there appears to be a purely practical knowledge, that is, one without any speculative or theoretical assumptions or implications. Practical knowledge is no more entirely useful than speculative knowledge is entirely useless. For example, one may have expert practical knowledge in how to construct water wheels, but in an age of atomic reactors such "useful" practical knowledge might better be described as useless.

One might also take examples of theoretical knowledge which is far from useless from physical science or from mathematics. Thus Einstein's general theory of relativity had no immediate practical application at the time of its formulation. It was an attempt to formulate an understanding of the physical universe in accordance with the data provided by experiment, some of which data seemed to contradict the classical mechanics of Newton, then generally accepted by physicists. That the theory had little to do with the practical order may be seen from the fact that it was many years before it could in any way be verified. And yet Einstein's theory represented the theoretical basis for the development of the atomic bomb, with all the political and moral dilemmas which this powerful instrument, for good or for ill, has for mankind.

At the time, however, Einstein's purely speculative and theoretical musings were entirely useless, as was the system of logic which Hegel had so carefully founded and built up. Their speculations were not, however, without practical applications. The same is true of the theoretical meditations of pure mathematicians on number theory or on the binomial number system in the last century. Constructing a number theory with a base of two instead of ten was, at the time, an entirely useless, though perhaps engrossing, intellectual pursuit. There were no known practical applications. And yet it was exactly such pure mathematical speculation which provided the theoretical basis for the development of the electronic computer in our own age, with the vast social and economic implications which computers have. One might say that the speculations of the topologist, the modern geometer who deals with spaces of any number ("n . . .") of dimensions is a useless area of theoretical mathematics. And yet it may be that his studies will prove invaluable for space travelers of the future attempting to plot their course to distant planets.

It may be true to say that pure speculation represents useless knowledge. But if communism, the atomic bomb, or the computer represent practical problems for present-day man, as well as challenges and possibilities for him, then the theoretical and speculative ideas which stood behind these realities cannot be understood as totally useless. From this it is clear that we cannot speak of purely speculative knowledge in the sense that there would be no possible practical application whatsoever. This does not mean that there is no distinction between practical and speculative knowing, between useful and useless knowledge. Practical knowledge is immediately useful in the sense that it is ordained specifically toward the practical order, whereas speculative knowledge is not.

But there is no purely speculative knowledge in the sense that any and every practical application is impossible. In this sense speculative and theoretical knowledge is not so much useless as nonuseful, at least in any immediate sense. What makes it possible for the purely speculative to become practical is the simple fact that the speculative is drawn from the realm of the practical; and hence as a knowledge which has been worked out and worked over, interpreted into a new form, it can be reapplied to the practical.

We have suggested above that speculative or theoretical knowledge, for example metaphysics, is useless. In the eyes of the practical and pragmatic American this might serve to condemn it from the start. However, the American philosopher C. S. Peirce, the founder of the philosophy of pragmatism, once observed that there are always enough people around to study useful things, but it is the study of the useless which brings about the genuine advance of science (*Collected Papers,* 1.75–79). It is the useless pursuit of knowledge for its own sake, the interpretation of things and the understanding of man in his world and of his world which is, more often in the long run, the most useful.

There is, however, one peculiar characteristic about useless studies which it might be well to point out before leaving this topic; and that is the fact that they are all-absorbing. One might wonder about this curious psychological fact. Perhaps, because there is no immediate practical application to what is speculated or theorized about, an over-compensation of interest is generated, and even required, to make such apparently useless pursuits of sufficient concern to continue their pursuit. However, philosophy or metaphysics is not peculiar in this: the fine arts, or literature as well, represent useless pursuits, and yet they are very absorbing both for the artist and for his audience: the play of sports is useless, and yet all-engrossing both for spectators and participants. Some of the most enjoyable pursuits that man indulges himself in are, from a purely practical point of view, useless. They are the fruit of a leisure which man has achieved through his increasing mastery of the practical order. And they are the most absorbing, and, as we have suggested, also the most rewarding, since in the longer run they may be the most productive, because they do, in fact, lead to an increase in the practical benefits for man, even though this may not be in any way obvious at the time. What is suggested here is that it is useless speculation, not necessity, which is the mother of invention.

8. SUMMARY

In this introductory section we have been concerned to show what it is that metaphysics deals with. Beginning with a review of the various names attached to the subject, we proceeded to a consideration of the various questions which might be posed regarding the general subject of our study. All of the interrogative words used to pose the question seemed in one way or another, disadvantageous as the opening gambit into our subject. But by retranslating the "What is being?" question of Aristotle into "What is a being?" we found in the analysis of one of the necessary constitutes of a being, namely existence or being, an access into our subject.

Being, it was seen, is not a concept, nor can it be defined conceptually. But since it is not perceived directly by the senses, the question of how it is known had to be considered. It was suggested that being is known as that which is most fundamentally "taken for granted" and, therefore, necessarily included in all that is, in fact, known. Finally, the distinction between speculative and practical knowing was treated; and it was suggested, drawing parallels from other theoretical areas of human knowledge, that metaphysics is not as useless a knowledge, that is, without implications and consequences, as it might at first sight appear. To this was added the point that "useless" pursuits such as philosophy, the arts, or even sports, have the peculiar psychological characteristic of being all-absorbing, perhaps because they are not really as useless as they may at first sight appear.

exercises

1. Discuss the word "metaphysics."
2. Contrast the Greek and post-Renaissance view of "nature."
3. Discuss the word "ontology."
4. What does it mean to say that metaphysics studies everything, and nothing?
5. What is the problem regarding questions and answers?
6. Discuss some of the ways in which the question about being might be posed, noting the disadvantages of any two of the questions.
7. What is the difficulty involved in asking the question "What is being?"
8. Discuss the use of the verb "is."
9. Being is not a quality or a predicate. Discuss.
10. How it is possible for Hegel to look upon being and nothing as the same?
11. Why do we normally ignore being?
12. Characterize and exemplify the difference between practical and speculative knowledge.
13. Is philosophy, and more specifically metaphysics, a purely speculative knowing?
14. Why is the useless all-absorbing?

bibliography

Anderson, J. F. "Some Disputed Questions on Our Knowledge of Being," *Review of Metaphysics,* 11 (1958) 550–568.

Aristotle. *Metaphysics,* Bks. IV, VI, VII, 1; XI, 1–7.

Ayer, A. J. *Language, Truth and Logic.* 2 ed.; New York: Dover, 1946, ch. I: "The Elimination of Metaphysics."

Bergson, Henri. "Philosophical Intuition," *The Creative Mind,* tr. M. L. Andison. New York: Wisdom Library Paperbacks, 1946, pp. 107–129.

Bossart, William. "Metaphysical Experience," *Review of Metaphysics,* 15 (1961) 34–50.

Bradley, F. H. *Appearance and Reality.* 2 ed.; Oxford: Clarendon Press, 1897, "Introduction."

Collingwood, R. G. *An Essay on Metaphysics.* Oxford: Clarendon Press, 1940, ch. VII: "The Reform of Metaphysics."

——. *The Idea of Nature.* Fair Lawn, N. J.: Galaxy Books, 1960, pp. 29–92.

Copleston, Frederick. *Contemporary Philosophy: Studies of Logical Positivism and Existentialism.* London: Burns & Oates, 1956, ch. V: "The Function of Metaphysics."

Ehman, R. R. "On the Possibility of Nothing," *Review of Metaphysics,* 17 (1963) 205–213.

Gilson, Etienne. *Being and Some Philosophers.* Toronto: Institute of Mediaeval Studies, 1952, ch. VI: "Knowledge and Existence," and Appendix.

——. *The Unity of Philosophical Experience.* New York: Scribners, 1937, ch. XII.

Heidegger, Martin. *An Introduction to Metaphysics,* tr. Ralph Manheim. New Haven, Conn.: Yale, 1959, ch. I.

——. "What is Metaphysics?" *Existence and Being,* ed. W. Brock. Chicago: Regnery Gateway, 1949.

Kant, Immanuel. *Critique of Pure Reason,* tr. N. K. Smith. New York: St. Martin's, 1956, pp. 503–506.

——. *Prolegomena to Any Future Metaphysics,* tr. L. W. Beck. New York: Liberal Arts, 1951, "Preamble."

Kierkegaard, Søren. *Concluding Unscientific Postscript,* tr. D. F. Swenson. Princeton, N. J.: Princeton, 1941, pp. 267–322.

Knight, T. S. "Why Not Nothing?" *Review of Metaphysics,* 10 (1956) 158–164.

Kuhn, Helmut. "Existence as a Philosophical Problem," *International Philosophical Quarterly,* 1 (1961) 367–389.

Marcel, Gabriel. *The Mystery of Being,* tr. R. Hague. Chicago: Gateway, 1960, vol. II, chs. I and II.

——. *Being and Having,* tr. Katharine Farrer. Glasgow: Glasgow University Press, pp. 9–43.

Maritain, Jacques. *Existence and the Existent,* tr. L. Galantiere and G. B. Phelan. Garden City, N. Y.: Doubleday Image, 1956, ch. I, pp. 20–55.

——. *Preface to Metaphysics*. New York: Sheed, 1939, Lectures I–III.

Moore, G. E. "Is Existence a Predicate?" *Philosophical Papers*. New York: Collier, 1962, pp. 114–125.

Owens, Joseph. *St. Thomas and the Future of Metaphysics*. Milwaukee: Marquette University Press, 1957.

Randall, J. H. "Metaphysics and Language," *Review of Metaphysics,* 20 (1967) 591–601.

II
BEING

In this second part we will be concerned to show what it means to speak of being as transcendental. It will then be necessary to give some more definite sense to being by showing that it is not necessarily unlimited or infinite, and how it is limited. This means discovering what it is that limits the being of a being. In this way it may be possible to show how each "a being" has a being of its own, and that this being would not necessarily be infinite. The notion of essence as limit would tend to pose certain problems as far as the being of God would be concerned, and these are taken up. A distinction is made between essence understood in a positive and in a negative sense; and this, in turn, leads to the statement of the two basic laws of metaphysics, namely the Laws of Essence and Existence. These laws are then subjected to various tests. There is a discussion of the sense in which one may say that essences exist, and a parallel is drawn with the way in which blindness may be said to exist. Again, the way in which being exists, namely transcendentally, is reviewed in the context of this testing of the basic laws. And finally the most critical test of the laws comes with the relation which being and a being would have with time.

1. BEING AS TRANSCENDENTAL

As we have seen above, there is one "element" or "quality" of a being which is all too often overlooked in any consideration of the "a being," namely its being, the fact that it *exists*. It is simply taken for granted. It was also noted that this particular "quality" or predicate is very different and unlike such qualities or predicates as orange, fibrous, and sweet. The quality or predicate of existence would be that without which any of the other qualities and predicates of the "a being" would not be at all. If Felix the cat did not exist, she would not *really* be black, furry, and purring. Already here we have one of the characteristic ways of being, namely the fact that being is an absolutely necessary condition for any qualities or characteristics possessed by the being that exists. For if Ranger were white and barking, but did not exist, then he would be something like the smile of the Cheshire cat in Lewis Carrol's *Alice in Wonderland* or the speech of a Ringwraith in J. R. R. Tolkien's *Lord of the Rings*. These are, however, fairy tales, and we read and enjoy them as such.

Existence is a very special kind of "predicate" or "quality," for without it none of the other predicates we might apply to a being would actually *be* those of a being, since without this "predicate" the "a being" would not be. When it was said that this is one of the "characteristic ways" of being, what was meant is that being is *transcendental*; and this is one of the meanings of being as transcendental, namely that it is an absolutely necessary condition without which the "a being" would not have any of the qualities it does, in fact, have, nor could we apply to it the predicates that we do in propositions and statements about it.

There are other meanings of the word transcendental as well. When we attempted to ask about this particular "quality," it was found that the question "What is being?" was a question which gave no answer; and one which, in the end, left being as vague and indeterminate as non-being or nothing. This occurred whenever we attempted to treat being or existence conceptually, or whenever we tried to consider being as though it were itself a concept. It could be "defined" conceptually only by means of non-being, which, by definition, does not exist. But there was another reason for denying that being or existence is merely a concept. In the first place, whatever existence a concept might be said to have—a question which we are leaving on the shelf until we get to the section on truth—the existence of Ranger could not merely be that of a concept. Kant was entirely correct in pointing out the disparity between being and concept, when he pointed out that being (taken as a concept) would add nothing to the concept we might have of a being or a thing. This is another meaning of being as transcendental: the being of a being does not and cannot exist merely as an abstract concept.

Being is transcendental in yet another sense. As was noted, I can see that the apple tree is blooming, smell the fragrance of its blossoms, and feel the roughness of its bark. There is, however, no way to see, smell, or feel the existence of the apple tree. Existence cannot be directly grasped by any one of the senses, or even by all the senses somehow taken together. Being or existence is something that "transcends" our normal sense experience, while at the same time representing the necessary condition for the sense experience of this particular existent thing in the first place. We can grasp the qualities of color, fragrance, and roughness with our senses, but not that of existence. It is impossible to put our finger on the blooming apple tree's existence, and yet we know that the tree does exist, otherwise there would be literally nothing there to put our finger on. This is the third meaning attached to transcendental.

What sort of "thing," then, is existence or being? It is clearly not concrete in the way that yonder blooming apple tree is a concretely existing tree. Yet neither is it abstract. The apple tree does not bloom or exist "in the abstract," but on the side of the hill. And although the existence of the blooming apple tree cannot be grasped directly by the senses or be defined conceptually, it does, however, make a difference. Existence represents the absolutely necssary condition for there being a blooming apple tree there at all, and having any of the qualities and predicates applied to it as something existing. The being or existence of a being is *transcendental*. It is not, of course, transcendental in the "out of this world" sense that Plato's Ideas are transcendental. Although it is not possible to put my finger on the existence of the apple tree somewhere within it, yet neither can its existence be said to exist in some primary or archetypal sense somewhere outside the apple tree. As we have seen, in respect to being, that is, to the being of a being, the question of "where's" is fundamentally ambiguous. One knows being or existence is there, not its exact "where."

2. BEING AS UNLIMITED

When we attempted to pose the question "What is being?", we found that an answer to this question, namely a concept of being, was simply not possible. For although we might make use of the concept non-dog (since there are actually such things as non-dogs, e.g., cats), in order to define the class of dog, we could not do this in the case of being. Non-being could define nothing; by definition, it does not exist. And to take being or non-being merely as concepts was to render them indistinguishable.

But if everything that is has being, and if there is no such "thing" as non-being to limit being, then clearly being is unlimited, unbounded, or infinite. For if we remove the circle from around being, since there would be no non-being to hold it within its bounds—non-being could hold nothing in—then it is clear that being is absolutely unlimited, all over the place, indistinguishable from the indeterminate vagueness of an abstract or pure non-being. And since there could be only one unbounded infinity, then being would also have to be identical with God, since if God would exist, infinity would presumably be one of his necessary properties. Infinite or unbounded being would, for all theoretical purposes, be the same as God; or, at least, there would be no way in which to distinguish the two, since each would represent an infinity. This would mean, further, that the existence or being of absolutely everything that would exist would also have to be God. Not even the most insignificant thing, the most apparently limited and finite "a being" that we might experience could be other than infinite. For if being is infinite, then there could be no finite parts to being; otherwise being would not, in fact, be infinite. To be infinite, except for some small parts that are finite, is not really to be infinite at all. And if infinite, being would also be divine; or at least there would be no way in which to distinguish existence or being from God. As was suggested earlier, this is a possible intellectual, or perhaps better, a religious option—to see the existence of each and every thing that exists as something divine and hence sacred.

However, an existence or being which would be totally unlimited and infinite, or identified with God in this way, without any qualification or limitation whatsoever, would be totally indefinite as well; it would be "all over the place." Being would be so vague in its infinite indefiniteness that it would not only be indistinguishable from God, but even, as Hegel's thought might suggest, indistinguishable (at least conceptually) from nothing or non-being as well.

But if one says that being and God are identical, then the existence or being of anything that exists is both divine and infinite also. One may be willing to say that man, or even the blooming apple tree, has about it something that is "divine"; however, it seems to run contrary to our experience of apple trees and like kinds of things to say that they are infinite. The apple tree seems very finite and limited in the things that it does and cannot do, that is, in the way it exists. For example, it does not bloom all year long. But if non-being cannot act as a limit to being since it does not exist, there must be something that does limit it.

3.   ESSENCE AS LIMIT

Most of the "a beings" that man experiences and comes into contact with appear as limited beings. They are limited by the laws of gravity; they are limited by other beings. But what of their existence? Is this finite and limited as well? And if so, how? What is it that provides the metaphysical foundation for the limitation of existence in "a beings" that are, in fact, limited. For a hint to the answer to this question we may return again to one of the questions we attempted to pose concerning being, namely Aristotle's question: *ti to on?* We have noted the disadvantages attendant upon the translation "What is being?" But what of the question "What is a being?" Since Ranger is a being, we may use him again as an example, and substitute "Ranger" for "a being" in the above question. And if we ask the question "What is Ranger?" the answer is simply "a dog." This is essentially what Ranger is. This is the *essence* of Ranger, essence meaning simply "what something is." This essence that Ranger has is not merely the conventional way in which we speak about him, conditioned as we are by the customs of language, nor is "dog" merely a logical genus or class, the way, for example, the word mammal is. There is something more to "dog" than this: Ranger really is a dog, physically, biologically, genetically, etc. It is possible, for example, to cross a dog of one species with that of another, and still get a dog. One cannot, however, cross a dog with a whale (though both are mammals) and get something like a dolphin. There is more to essence than merely arbitrary biological classification; in fact, all such basic biological classifications, if they would have any meaning, must be based upon the fact of essence. The same would be true of the chemical classification of elements. There is a particular "what" or essence (what something is) to a crystal of sodium chloride (table salt) very different from a crystal of paradichlorobenzene (moth balls). In this sense one may say that science truly depends upon, and rests its classifications and most basic laws on the fact of essence.

Thus, given the total absence of non-being as something to limit being, it is clearly essence that limits the being or existence of a being. This means that the being of a being is not necessarily infinite. Felix' existence is limited by essence to being no more and no less than the existence of a cat. Felix cannot, therefore, fly like a bird, nor can she do calculus problems like a college student. Her essence, namely what she is, limits the existence she has. Felix can be no more or less than what she is, and exactly in this manner is her being or existence limited and finite.

This may solve the problem of the identification of an unlimited or infinite being with an infinite God, since each and every "a being" has a being or existence that is limited by essence. Felix' existence would not be an infinite existence since it is made finite, that is, is limited, by essence, by what Felix is. But is this true of every being? Is every "a being" limited by essence, by the kind of being that it is? This would certainly be true of every "a being" that is, in fact, finite or limited. But would it also be true of an infinite being such as God would be? Would God's existence also be limited by his essence? If by essence we mean limit upon existence, could one even say that God has an essence? For if he had such a limiting essence, he would not be infinite? The question may appear outside the province of metaphysics strictly speaking, and in the area of what is sometimes called natural theology. However, unless it is in some way resolved, the finite and limited existence of Felix may not really be finite and limited after all.

For if God would not have an essence, his existence would be infinite in the sense of "all over the place," and there would be no way of being sure whether Felix' existence were not (secretly) God's; there would be no way to be sure that God was not in some way identical with the being of each and every "a being" that existed, vaguely everywhere without any meaning given to that everywhere. And yet to limit God's existence would appear to deny his infinity, which is understood traditionally as one of the properties of divine existence. It would be to no advantage to say that God's limiting essence is simply infinity, that is, to be unlimited. To say that the limit of something is to be unlimited; or to say that God, an unlimited being, limits himself to being unlimited could only be meaningless and a contradiction in terms.

4. ASPECTS OF ESSENCE

We must, of course, return to the meaning attached to the word essence, if this difficulty regarding the essence of God, and the genuinely finite existence of limited things, is to be resolved, at least in a preliminary way. We have understood the word essence primarily as "what something is," and noted that it is essence that limits existence. One might, however, argue that essence would limit being or existence only in a finite being, not in an infinite being. And further, and more fundamentally, one might question whether the notion of limitation is the primary and basic meaning of essence. Limitation concentrates on the negative, on what something is *not*, rather than on what something *is*. A limit sets bounds: no more and no less. In this connection it is possible to run down a list of what something, for example Ranger, is not. He is not a fish, not a bird, a whale, a man, etc. The list of things that Ranger is not, and hence the things that he cannot do, that is, swim like a fish, fly like a bird, do calculus problems, etc., could extend indefinitely. One might say that this is considering essence *negatively*, that is, from the point of view of what something is not: what something is not more or less than, to put the matter in a somewhat cumbersome fashion. This is clearly not the most basic meaning of essence. We recognize it immediately as a very inefficient and roundabout approach for determining what Ranger actually is—not an elephant, not an ant, etc. Clearly, it would take forever to catalog all the things that a particular thing is not. And besides, Ranger is limited in his being or existence by essence, not by the thousand and one things that he is not. There may be other beings or things that limit a being, but the being or existence of a being is limited by essence, not by those thousand and one things that may, in fact, limit it.

And in any case, it is not essence understood negatively which determines what Ranger is not, but rather essence understood *positively*, namely as "what he is." This is the basis metaphysically for saying that Ranger is not a cat, not a bird, not an elephant, etc. Ranger is not any of these kinds of things because he is, first and foremost, what he is, namely a dog. Everything that he is not depends upon the fact that he is no more and no less than what he is. It is essence, taken in this positive sense, which accounts for our ability to say, negatively, what something is not.

If we return to the case of God, and to one of the properties traditionally applied to him, namely infinity, we find something curious. The very term "infinity" is itself already an essence taken negatively (*in-fines*, having no bounds or limits). Hence, in one of the very words used to describe God's essence we use a term which

designates "what he is not," namely non-finite, unlimited. But because every negative determination must depend upon a positive
one, we do not thereby say that God does not have a positive essence,
but merely that we do not necessarily know what that essence is; and
we acknowledge this implicitly in using this negative word to describe his essence. This does not mean that God would be limited by
what he is not (by Ranger, by me, by evil, etc.); rather, he would be
what he is. God, then, would have an essence. He will not, as we
shall see, violate the Law of Essence. If God did not have an essence, he would not be the being that he is, but some other being;
and, in the end, his being would be indistinguishable from that of
every other existing being, particularly if he were infinite, and, for
that matter, from nothing or non-being, as we saw above in the case
of absolutely unlimited being. This does not necessarily mean that
it would be possible to know what the essence of God would be,
taken in a positive sense. And this is, perhaps, the reason why we
tend to use negative determinations in describing that essence. But
if God did not have an essence in a positive sense, then he would not
be what he is, but what he is not, which is meaningless and absurd.
It may be true that man, a finite being, can use only negative determinations in speaking and thinking about an infinite being; but one
might argue that he could do even this only if there were a positive
essence to such a being.

In all this we are not attempting to prove the existence of God,
nor are we assuming that existence. Metaphysics cannot, indeed, dis-
prove the existence of God or give metaphysical grounds for his
nonexistence. One can, of course, argue that God cannot be grasped
either conceptually or perceptually; however, the same is true, as we
have seen, of being or existence. Being is no more an abstract concept than God would be; neither can being be grasped directly by
the senses. But in the same way that it is not possible to argue that
being does not exist simply because it is not grasped perceptually or
conceptually—though if there were no such "thing" as being, there
would be literally nothing to be grasped—so also in the case of God.
God would seem to have the same transcendental status as being.
Hence, although it may not be the task of metaphysics to prove the
existence of God, still metaphysics must admit the possibility of such
an existence, since it must admit the "existence" of its own object of
study. This is why even in a strictly metaphysical consideration of

being the existence of God must at least be taken into account. It must be taken into account if only because, were God not to have an essence, for example, there would be literally no way to determine whether the existence or being of every thing that does, in fact, exist would not be the existence of God. This latter possibility must be ruled out if we wish to insist that each and every "a being" has a being of its own, and if we wish to avoid one of the cruder forms of pantheism.

5. LAWS OF ESSENCE AND EXISTENCE

We are now in a position to establish our first laws of metaphysics. If metaphysics would, indeed, be a science, then it must concern itself with establishing certain laws of general validity regarding the subject with which it deals. Thus we have seen that every "a being" that exists has and must have both essence and being or existence. All finite beings are constituted of an essence which limits its existence to being a certain kind of thing. Even an infinite being, as we have seen, must have an essence in a positive sense, even though we may be unable fully to understand what that essence might be, or to describe it in anything but negative terms.

The laws thus established are those of essence and existence:

LAW OF ESSENCE: A thing (or a being) cannot be without being a certain kind of thing (or being).
LAW OF EXISTENCE: A thing (or a being) cannot be a certain kind of thing (or being) without being.

These laws will apply to any existing thing or being. They are meant to emphasize the fact that every thing, or "a being," must have both these necessary constituents. Ranger exists; but he can exist only as a certain kind of being or thing. Ranger is not an essence; he is not Dog, with a capital "D." There are other dogs besides Ranger, e.g., Fido. And even if Ranger were the last of a vanishing species, he would still not exhaust the possibilities of being a dog. No essence of a finite thing, since it would necessarily imply an essence limiting that being, could possibly be infinite. Thus even if Ranger were absolutely unique, that is, the only one of its kind, he would still not exhaust infinitely the possibilities of being a dog. And to view him as the single member of a logical class which he entirely fills would require us to take a purely abstract and logical view of Ranger. But as we have seen, the existence of Ranger is not that of a concept, nor can it be reduced to an abstract concept.

But if Ranger and Fido are both dogs, that is, if both have the same essence, and if they both exist, then how can they be said to differ? Clearly, if the laws of essence and existence are correct, that is, if there is a necessary correlation between essence and existence, and if there are no other basic metaphysical constituents to things (and no others have thus far been discovered), then the only way in which Ranger and Fido might be said to differ would be on the score of their existence. But do not Ranger and Fido both exist? How could they be said to differ over the matter of existence? Although it is, indeed, true that both Ranger and Fido exist, still they do not have the same existence. For if Ranger and Fido had the same existence, as well as the same essence, then from a metaphysical point of view they would have to be the same dog. There would not be two dogs, but one. For if both had the same essence and the same existence, there would be absolutely no difference between the two. Ranger would be Fido, and Fido Ranger. They would be the same dog.

Another indication that it is over the matter of existence that Ranger and Fido differ is the fact that they cannot exchange existences. Each exists; but each has an existence of his own. Each has an existence which is limited in essentially the same way—both can only exist as dogs—but it is not the same existence that is thus limited, but two different existences. One may speak of two things of the same kind possessing or "sharing" the same essence, though there are ambiguities in such a manner of speaking; but one cannot speak of two things possessing or sharing the same existence, even in the case of a symbiotic relationship. For although two dissimilar organisms live in a close association mutually advantageous, there are two dissimilar organisms; even though both might perish if separated. If the existences of Ranger and Fido were not irrevocably their own, so long as they existed, we might have a great deal of difficulty in approaching a peaceful, cowardly dog such as Ranger; today he might have the existence of the mean and vicious Fido. Something exchanging existences with something else occurs only in fairy tales, which, insofar as they are, by definition, fictional (that is, unreal) have nothing essentially to do with metaphysics.

There are, however, several ways in which we may test the validity of the laws we have discovered and formulated; and in the application of these laws something of their meaning, and correlatively the meaning of being, may come clearer.

a. Do Essences Exist?

At first sight the question "Do essences exist?" would seem to require an affirmative answer. After all, if there are beings that exist, and if each "a being" must have essence and being, in accordance with the universal Laws of Essence and Existence, then in this sense essences must exist.

However, we must be a little more cautious. For if whatever exists must have essence and existence, in accordance with the laws, then if we say that essences exist, that is, if we say that an essence is a being, then that "a being" (namely, that essence) must have essence and being as well. Similarly, that essence of the original essence (if essences exist) must also have essence and being; and further, the essence of the essence of the essence, etc., must also have being, and so on *ad infinitum*. We are thus left with an infinity of essences or with an infinite world of essences, each one of which would also have essence and being. All this would follow if we say that essences do, in fact, exist. And this is most certainly a metaphysical option; but it is a very "messy" one, and one which does not seem justified by the facts. Indeed, it seems to result in a multiplication of entities in a sort of cornucopian fashion beyond all necessity and beyond every possibility of putting a stop to the infinite and inexhaustible flow. It also tends to make the work of metaphysics unnecessarily difficult, if not impossible; for this infinity of existing essences would be beyond the possibility of finite investigation.

Other difficulties are posed if we say that essences exist. For example, where was Fido's essence, that of dog, lodged or located before Fido began to exist? Or what happens to that essence when he ceases to exist? If essences exist, where does the essence of Fido go when he dies? Does it, perhaps, pass on to the Great Dog Heaven in the sky? On the other hand, how could an essence be said to die? For even though Fido should die, there would still be other dogs around to keep the essence dog "alive." More than likely, the question is an incorrect one: rather than asking where Fido's essence was before he existed, or where that essence goes when he ceases to exist, one should probably rather ask: "Did that essence ever really exist in the first place?" And as we have seen above, in order for it to exist, it must be a being. But if it is a being, then that essence must have essence and being, which essence must, in turn, have essence and being, etc.

Clearly essences do not exist in the way that beings exist, any more than do essences exist in the same way that being itself "exists" —*what* something is must be distinguished from the fact *that* something is. Nevertheless, essence is one of the necessary constituents of a being, and thus must exist in some way. Certainly Fido's essence does not exist in such a way that it might survive the demise of Fido, any more than it existed prior to Fido's existence or prior to the appearance of the animal species dog. Still, essences do exist as the necessary constituents of existing things, since in limited and finite "a beings" essence limits the being of that "a being" to being this particular kind of thing. But then how do essences exist? Since the negative meaning of essence as limitation is not the primary meaning for essence, but rather the positive meaning of "what something is," then to what might we compare essence in order to bring out its peculiar meaning? We might, perhaps, draw a parallel with blindness in respect to a being, and thereby indicate something of the kind of existence essence would have in respect to existence.

b.   Essence and the Parallel of Blindness

In his short work *On Being and Essence,* Thomas Aquinas speaks of blindness as a "privation," that is, as a lack of something (in this case the power of sight) which should be there. One speaks of a blind dog as one "deprived" of sight. One does not speak of a mole as so deprived; moles are not expected to be able to see. As something of which the dog is deprived, one might look upon blindness as really a "nothing." However, it would certainly not appear as "nothing at all" to the blind dog itself; for it would be a "nothing" that would force a drastic change in the basic modes and normal patterns of the dog's life and behavior. And this is the first consideration that must be borne in mind in any consideration of a privation, that is of something negative, like blindness: it is clearly not something abstract or conceptual, a mere idea. It may be a lack, that is, a sort of nothing; but it is a very concrete sort of lack, a very real sort of "nothing." But if it is something concrete, and something very real for the being thus deprived, one might wonder whether it is, in fact, a being.

In order to answer this question we are forced back to our Laws of Essence and Existence. Clearly blindness does not have existence in the same way that the blind dog has essence and existence. It is, rather, a lack of "something" that should be there; it is nonexistence rather than existence. But since such a privation does not have "existence" independent of a being which actually does exist—there is no blindness something existing independently of beings that are blind —one might look upon blindness as a sort of Aristotelian "accident," that is, something that inheres in, or literally "goes along with," the substance. The difficulty with this view is that a privation would be a very peculiar sort of accident in Aristotle's sense of that word. The fact that Fido is black in color and large in size might be understood as "accidents" to Fido's substance. However, being blind, that is, being without the ability to see (whereas most other dogs have the power of sight as a normal way of their being), would be a very different sort of accident. It would be a "negative accident," a very odd sort of accident indeed; since most accidents to substance are positive rather than negative in meaning.

Similarly, if one were to say that blindness is something existing, then it would also have to possess an essence. It might appear as though blindness does have an essence, in that we are able to talk about it. But upon closer examination we find that we talk about blindness only in negative terms, that is, a lack of sight. Blindness might be said to have an essence only in this negative sense, and hence not in the positive sense; however, it is this positive sense which would have to be primary in the case of essence, and this is not the situation with blindness. It is possible to speak of blindness only in the sense of its opposite, the positive power or quality of being able to see.

Clearly, then, blindness does not exist in the strict sense. It is not a being, since it lacks both essence and existence. Neither does it exist in a being as a sort of "negative quality." It does, however, represent a limit, but not a limit to existence, as does essence, but rather a limit to a being, as in the case of a limited being such as Fido. And here lies the value of this digression into the meaning of a privation for an understanding of the kind of "existence" that an essence has. In the same way that the existence of a being is limited by essence, so Fido, as a being, is limited by the privation of blindness. Taken by itself essence would have only a negative significance. But, in accordance with our Law of Existence, essence can never exist in such a fashion. This is why essence can have the positive meaning and significance that it has, namely as "what something is." It is only on this positive basis that essence can have the negative meaning of limit that it does. This can also be seen in the parallel with blindness. Understood merely as the lack of sight, the meaning of such a privation is essentially negative. But as the privation of a being that does exist, it also has a very definite positive meaning and significance.

But although there are significant parallels between the meaning of blindness in relation to a being and the kind of "existence" an essence has in relation to being or existence, the primacy of the positive and the negative is different in each case. The meaning of a privation is essentially negative; whereas the primary meaning of essence in a being that exists is fundamentally positive.

c.   Does Being Exist?

This question is similar to the one we asked in relation to essence. And like the previous question its value lies in the light that it throws upon being itself, and the test which the question makes of the validity of our Laws of Essence and Existence. The question may, at first sight, seem a curious one. For if what we are considering in this course is being, then it must certainly exist. In fact, one of the basic "assumptions" of the course was that there is something that does exist. Hence, being must exist.

However, in accordance with our Laws of Essence and Existence, in order for being to exist, it would have to have both essence and being. To exist being would have to be a being. One problem is immediately obvious: Ranger is a being, but as we have seen, although it is possible to sense Ranger, it is not possible, in any direct fashion, to sense Ranger's being. Furthermore, to say that existence has existence would appear to be grammatically redundant, that is, unless the kind of existence that being might have would be better determined. And to determine "what kind of" existence being might have would seem to involve us in the question of the essence, the "what," of being or existence; and, as we have also seen, being or existence cannot have a "what." For although it is true that *a* being has an essence (limiting its existence), it would not be correct to say that the *being* of a being has an essence. Essence is not something which being has, but something that *a* being has. The being of a being does not have an essence; rather, essence is that whereby the being of a being is limited to being this particular kind of being. Likewise, essence is not something that being is, since if being were an essence then it would be the only one; and we would find ourselves back in the large circle of being, such as may be experienced in Parmenides (cf. Appendix I, Section 2). Clearly, then, being or existence does not exist, since what exists are "a beings," having essence and being. And being is not a being, since it has no essence, nor is it an essence, but is limited by one. Finally, being does not have existence; being *is* existence. There is no distinction between being and existence. But there is a distinction between being and *a* being. The latter has, necessarily, both essence and being. Hence, being or existence does not exist.

This line of argument can produce nothing more than the conclusion that being is not a being, which, since being is one of the necessary, and absolutely necessary constituents of a being, should come as no surprise. For if there are beings that exist, then there must be existence or being. But one may go further: if there are things that exist, then there *must be* existence or being. For if a being does not have the "quality" of being, then it cannot have all the other qualities and characteristics which the "a being" has, and which we predicate of it. Thus although there is a distinction between being and a being, there is also a necessary interrelationship. There are things that exist only if there is being or existence. If there are things, then there is being; indeed, being then *must be*. Likewise, being exists only if there are things or beings having essence and being.

Then could being exist, if there were not things? For example, before there were things (if one could, indeed, speak of a "before" in such a context), was there just being? Or if all things should cease to exist in some cosmic cataclysm, would being cease to exist? The questions introduce the element of time, which will occupy us at some length in the following section. But even at this point it can be insisted that the questions are hypothetical. This means that they are not concerned primarily with what, in fact, exists, but with what might be or with what might have been. As such, they fall outside the purview of metaphysics. All that can be said is that if there are beings that exist, then being exists as well, and this by necessity. But this does not mean that being exists as *a* being, for reasons we have seen above. Then how, one might ask, does it exist?

In order to describe the way in which being exists it is necessary to use a technical term, whose meaning has already been delineated earlier when we spoke of being as transcendental. The way in which being "exists" is *transcendentally*. This means, first of all, that being exists as an absolutely necessary condition for a being, for all the qualities and characteristics which that "a being" may have, and for all the properties that may be predicated of it. Thus, the carrot would not have the qualities of orange, fibrous, and sweet if it were not a being; and it would not be a being unless it had the more basic and fundamental quality of being or existence.

The other meanings of "existing transcendentally" are largely negative in character. The way in which being exists is not as an abstract concept. In this connection we have seen that the concept will in no wise get us into contact with being. Such concepts are based primarily on essence; and as we have seen, being does not have an essence: it is limited by an essence. Being does not have an essence, nor is it an essence. If it were an essence it would be the only essence. Literally every-thing would be being, and all things would have the same "what," namely being. Finally, being exists transcendentally in the sense that it is not something which can be grasped directly by any of the senses. Being is something necessarily real, and yet the being of the carrot is not concrete and sensible in the way that the carrot is itself concrete and sensible.

Being does, then, exist. It exists transcendentally. It does not exist as a being, since it does not have an essence. And it is this fact that brings out the sharp distinction between being and a being. Being is not a being; nor is a being, being. A being does exist, but it does not exhaust the possibilities of existence. But although there is an "ontological difference between Being (*das Sein*) and the being (*das Seiende*)," as Heidegger insists; or, as was indicated by Aquinas, between "to be" (*esse*) or the "act of existing" (*actus essendi*) and being (*ens*) or thing (*res*), there is also a necessary and reciprocal relation between the two. Indeed, without being there would be no beings that exist; however, if there were not things or "a beings," there would be no being either. This means simply that the transcendental character of being is not such that it can be considered somehow independently of actually existing things, as though it might be transferred or imagined as existing in some Platonic heaven. Being exists transcendentally, in the sense that we have delineated above; nonetheless, it does not follow from this that the being of a being exists so transcendentally that it would be totally outside the world in which those things actually do exist.

6. DOES BEING HAVE ANYTHING TO DO WITH TIME?

Being exists; it exists transcendentally. But it can be said to exist only if there are things which actually do exist. If there are things, then there is being. One may go even further: if there are things, then there *must be* being, since, as transcendental, being represents an absolutely necessary condition for any-thing being at all. Given this reciprocal dependence of being upon things, and things upon being, one might wonder about the relation between being and time. Some things are, in any case, temporal; they have a great deal to do with time. But if the existence of being, albeit existing transcendentally, depends upon things or beings, and these, or at least some of them, are temporal, then does not being also have something to do with time?

In the first place, one might ask why the question of the relation between time and being should have become so important in contemporary metaphysics. It was not always so. In earlier philosophical periods, time was generally treated in the area known as natural philosophy. Thus Aristotle, for example, treated time in his

Physics as one of the accidents of substance, defining time as the measure of motion, but not as part of any consideration of being as being. Thus one might well wonder how and why time should have come to be considered within the confines of metaphysics, as it is, for example, in the philosophies of Bergson and Heidegger. One might, of course, simply say that the reason for this lies in the fact that natural philosophy, or the philosophy of nature in the old sense, was supplanted by modern science or by the new physics that arose with Copernicus, Galileo, and Newton. Or one might say that it was the development of the historical disciplines and the application of history to every area of human study which prompted a new look at the phenomenon of time and its relation to being.

According to Samuel Alexander, Bergson was the first philosopher really to take time seriously. In Bergson this is no longer time understood simply as a property of physical bodies moving in space; being itself is understood temporally or as process. One might wonder why time should have become so central to a metaphysical endeavor. And the reason for this fact must be ascribed to the influence of Charles Darwin and the theory of evolution. For the theory of evolution introduced a new notion of change, and thereby forced philosophers to rethink the traditional view of time and its relation to being.

As is clear, a being, such as a race horse for example, has a great deal to do with time. For example, the horse can run the track and be clocked at such and such a time. This is basically the view of time taken by Aristotle as the measure of motion. But the race horse also has something to do with time in that while he is moving or running around the track he is also changing; this we note when we say that he is growing older and can no longer participate in races for three-year-olds. We are able to note the time involved in the metabolic processes, whereby the horse is able to live, against a certain set standard, for example, the periodic revolutions of the earth around the sun, which constitutes the earth's year. Thus are we able to say that the race horse is so many years old. In order to know how much time a particular "a being" has lived relative to other things in existence, we set that being's time against a certain standard for measuring time.

But against what standard might we set being in order to determine its time, thus to discover whether being as such is temporal or not? There is simply no vantage point or frame of reference we might use, or from which we might "time" being or establish its temporality. One might, of course, set the time of being against the eternity of God. However, since by eternity we mean what is nontemporal, and since what is nontemporal could be understood only in relation to what is temporal, this would be of little assistance. For the very notion of eternity is generally extrapolated from one or the other of the dimensions of time, and then idealized. Eternity is either an everlasting concretized present (the *nunc stans* of Boethius) or it is an infinite past and future (the spatialization of time into an absolute "always was and always will be").

The only "thing" other than being against which being might be set to determine its temporality would be nothing or non-being. However, non-being could hardly act as a measure or standard against which to set anything, since, by definition, non-being does not exist. One might, of course, deny that time has anything whatsoever to do with being. However, this would be to understand being in such a "transcendental" way that it would be totally outside the temporal order of existing things which have being. It would also tend to put time totally outside being, indistinguishable from nothing. This is, indeed, one way of obviating the problem of the relation between time and being: simply deny that there is any such thing as time. Indeed, some metaphysicians have taken this option, for example Parmenides. And other philosophers, for example Plato, have placed an eternal and unchangeable being so far removed from the temporal order of things as to make the problem irrelevant.

One might, of course, attempt to ascertain the "time" of being by means of that of the thing. But although there is a reciprocal relation between being and thing, such that there can be a thing only if there is being—being exists (transcendentally, indeed) only if there are things—still, there is also a fundamental difference between being and thing. As we have seen, a being has essence and being; whereas being does not.

Now if we say that time in a being is based upon change, in the same way that its measurement is based upon motion, then one might ask which one of the two necessary metaphysical constituents of a being, essence or existence, is it that changes when the "a being" does, in fact, change? What is responsible for the change in a being? Clearly a being or thing can and does change; but what is it in the "a being" that changes? Clearly essence does not change; Ranger does not cease to be a dog simply because he loses a part of his ear in a fight with Fido. It may, of course, be true that the changes which take place in Ranger can take place only within the limits of the essence which he does, in fact, possess. Thus, for example, Ranger cannot change from a dog into a cat in order to climb trees in pursuit of Felix. The kind of changes which occur in a being must occur within the limit of the essence that it has.

One might, of course, object that we have examples of such essential change in the history of evolution, and it is, perhaps, the fact of such essential changes over long periods of evolutionary time which introduced the question of the relation between time and being into metaphysics, as was suggested above. But although it may, indeed, be true that evolutionary change from one generation to the next represents an essential change, from a fish to an amphibian for example, in metaphysics we are primarily concerned with what actually exists. And what exists is "a beings" having essence and existence. And the essence of a being, as *what* it, in fact, is, cannot itself change. Indeed, mutations can occur in a fertilized egg, for example, meaning that the offspring may be different than the parent species. However, this represents the genesis of another "a being," and hence a new existence limited by an essence. The essence of Fido cannot change so long as Fido exists; he can only exist as a dog. He can cease to be a dog only be ceasing to exist, that is, by ceasing to be Fido.

But if essence does not change in a being that is already constituted of essence and being, then one might say that it is the being or existence of a being that changes. Given the fact that "a beings" do, in fact, change; and given also the absolutely necessary condition that being is the existence of a being, and if essence does not change, then it must be the being or existence of a being that changes. There are, however, certain difficulties in taking this position. To say that the being of a being changes would mean that there was some alteration or modification of its existence. Being cannot, however, change partially, since existence is not something which a being can have only partially. A thing cannot half exist. It either has existence or it does not. One might call this the All or None Law, a law discovered in the very beginning of metaphysics by Parmenides: either it is or it is not.

If the being of a being cannot change partly or partially, in accordance with all the All or None Law, then neither could it change as a whole. The only "thing" that being could change into would be something which it is not already, and that would be non-being. Normally, however, we use the word change to mean a modification or alteration of something into something else. A change from something into nothing or non-being would represent a very curious notion of change indeed. Ceasing to exist would be a change too radical to be called a change. This is why for a change of this magnitude we reserve the word "annihilation." For given the dependece of being upon a being for its existence, the simple ceasing to be of a being would represent a change from which no further changes could possibly be expected, at least so far as that "a being" would be concerned.

From the above, it would appear that metaphysics cannot account for the fact of change, and hence for time. For although the metaphysician must admit that beings do, in fact, change, he must deny that the fundamental constitutive elements of a being, that is, essence and existence, do themselves change. However, the fact that the existence or the being of a being does not itself change does not mean that being has nothing whatsoever to do with change, and therefore with time. After all, being is something that certain finite and limited beings or things possess *in time*. Hence, being must have some relation to things that change in time, since being is the absolutely necessary condition for the thing's existing in the first place.

Clearly, being must have something to do with time; and yet, although the being that changes is made up of essence and being, neither essence or being in a being that exists can themselves change. It is true, as we have seen above, that change in a being takes place within the limits of the essence of the thing, which essence, as we have also seen, limits the existence of the thing. But then what of the relation between time and change and being? Being is not itself temporal, since it does not change. Then what is the basis for change in a being that does, in fact, change? Change could not find its basis in essence, since essence is only the limits within which change would take place. Change, and therefore time as well, could only find its basis in existence, given the fact of change in a being, having essence and being; and given also the absolutely necessary condition that being is for a being. This means that although being does not change, it is, nevertheless, the basis for change in a being that does change. Being is not, then, itself temporal, even though it is the basis for time in a being that is temporal.

This may appear as a far from satisfactory conclusion: to say that being does not change, and hence is not temporal; and yet to say that it is the basis for change in a being that does change and its temporal. Such a solution may appear anomalous or paradoxical. It appears to make existence, or the being of a being, in some way nontemporal. A more accurate assessment would, however, be to say that being is neither necessarily temporal nor nontemporal (that is, eternal), but a-temporal; in the same way that one may speak of a person as neither moral nor immoral, but amoral: the categories of ethics are simply not made directly or personally applicable. For it is not possible to say that being has, necessarily, nothing to do with time or with change, any more than it is possible to say that it does necessarily have something to do with time or change. After all, being is the absolutely necessary condition for the existence of the individual being which does, in fact, change. Hence, it is not possible to say that being has nothing whatsoever to do with time, any more than it is possible to say that the amoral person *necessarily* has nothing to do with morality. In the first place, we clearly speak of such a person as a-moral; and secondly, the fact that the amoral person does not recognize moral obligation does not mean that there is none, or that he or she may not discover moral obligation sometime in the future. Similarly in the case of being and its relation to time: being can be the basis for change, and hence for the temporal, in a being that changes and is temporal, even though the being of the "a being" does not itself change, and hence is not itself temporal.

It may, of course, appear somewhat paradoxical to conclude that a being is indeed temporal, whereas its being is not; particularly, when we consider the reciprocal relation between being and a being. However, this is exactly the point: a being depends *upon* being for its being, and hence can the being of that "a being" operate as the basis for change in it, even though being does not itself change. In fact, if the being of a thing did, indeed, change, then it could hardly provide a stable foundation for the change which actually does occur in a being that does, in fact, change. Finally, paradoxical as it may seem to say that a being is temporal, while its being is not, this is no more paradoxical than saying that a being is sensible, whereas its being is not, as we were forced to say above. In any science there are matters which may seem strange or paradoxical; but this does not necessarily make them any the less true, particularly if they follow from principles which are known to be true.

7.   SUMMARY

In this section we have tried to show what it means to say that being exists transcendentally; namely, that it exists as a necessary condition for a being, that it does not exist as a concept, and that it is not directly sensible. We were also concerned to dispose of the possibility that the existence of a finite "a being" is not that of God by indicating what it is, namely essence, that limits the being of a being so that it is the "a being's" own. The meaning of essence as limit was outlined; but it was then noticed that the more negative meaning of essence as limit finds its basis in the positive significance of essence as "what something is." This makes it possible to speak of God as a being, so that if he would exist he would not violate our fundamental metaphysical Laws of Essence and Existence.

It was shown that essences do not, strictly speaking, exist, except as one of the necessary constituents of a being. The kind of "existence" essences would have in relation to being was compared with the kind of existence that blindness would have to a being deprived of sight. Finally, the question of the relation of being and time was considered. It was found, after suggesting the way in which the whole question of time entered metaphysics, that there is really no way to "time" being. If time in a being is a function of change, then it became a question of determining which of the two metaphysical constituents of a being, namely essence or being, would change to account for change in the thing that does, in fact, change. It was argued that neither essence nor being does change. However, change in a being can take place only within the limits of essence; and although the being of a being does not itself change, existence or being does constitute the necessary basis for any change in a being, simply because being is the absolutely necessary condition for the existence

of the "a being." This discussion of the relation between time and
being led, incidentally, to the formulation of another law in metaphysics, namely the All or None Law, which will prove extremely
helpful in the following section dealing with the first of the transcendental properties of being, namely one.

exercises

1. What does it mean to say that being is transcendental?
2. Indicate some of the consequences if being is not limited.
3. How is being limited? Discuss.
4. Does the limitation of being leave any unsolved difficulties? Indicate them. How might they be resolved?
5. Discuss the distinction between essence in its positive and negative aspects.
6. Give the Laws of Essence and Existence. What is their principal implication so far as they are related to each other?
7. How do two things having the same essence differ?
8. Do essences exist? If so, why? If not, why not?
9. What sort of "thing" is blindness? Discuss its parallel with essence.
10. Does being exist? How not? How so?
11. Why has the question of time and its relation to being entered metaphysics?
12. Compare change and time in a being with the possibility of change in essence.
13. Could being change, such that it might be said to be temporal?
14. How, then, are the necessary metaphysical constituents of a being related to change and thence to time?

bibliography

Aquinas, Thomas. *On Being and Essence,* tr. Armand Maurer. Toronto: Institute of Mediaeval Studies, 1949.

Aristotle. *Metaphysics,* VII, 11–12, 14; XI, 10–11.

Bergson, Henri. *An Introduction to Metaphysics,* tr. T. E. Hulme. New York: Liberal Arts, 1955.

Carlo, W. E. "The Role of Essence in Existential Metaphysics," *International Philosophical Quarterly,* 4 (1964) 557–590.

Clark, W. N. "What is Really Real?" *Progress in Philosophy*. Milwaukee: Bruce, 1955, pp. 61–90.

Collingwood, R. G. *The Idea of Nature*. Fair Lawn, N. J.: Galaxy Books, 1960, pp. 93–177.

Fabro, Cornelio. "The Transcendentality of *Ens-Esse* and the Ground of Metaphysics," *International Philosophical Quarterly*, 6 (1966) 389–427.

Gilson, Etienne. *Being and Some Philosophers*. 2 ed.; Toronto: Institute of Mediaeval Studies, 1952, chs. III and V.

Grabau, R. F. "Existence and Being," *Experience and Existence*, ed. I. C. Lieb. Carbondale, Ill.: Southern Illinois University Press, 1961.

Heidegger, Martin. *An Introduction to Metaphysics*, tr. Ralph Manheim. New Haven, Conn.: Yale, 1959, chs. II and III.

Imgarden, Roman. *Time and Modes of Being*, tr. H. R. Michejda. Springfield, Ill.: Thomas, 1964, pp. 99 ff.

Lovejoy, A. O. *The Great Chain of Being*. New York: Harper Torchbooks, 1960, esp. chs. I and II.

Phelan, G. B. "The Being of Creatures," *Proceedings of the American Catholic Philosophical Association*, 21 (1957) 118 ff.

Santayana, George. *Realms of Being*. New York: Scribner, 1942, Bk. I, chs. 2 and 4.

Spinoza. *Ethics*, Bk. I.

Weiss, Paul. "Being, Essence and Existence," *Review of Metaphysics*, 1 (1947) 69–92.

III
THE TRANSCENDENTALS

Once we have said that being exists, and indicated what is meant by the way in which it exists, namely transcendentally, one might ask whether this is all that can be said about being. It is true that being cannot be defined, for reasons we have seen above. However, when it is not possible to define something, it may be possible to describe it "in other words"; and where it is not possible even to describe what is before us, we may be able to compare the subject of discourse with something related to it, whether by similarity or contrast. In the case of being it is impossible to compare by contrast. Non-being simply does not exist. But what would being be related to by way of similarity?

Clearly, anything which would, like being, exist transcendentally could throw some light upon being. In other words, anything that would exist as a necessary condition for the positive qualities of a thing or a being, which was not able to be grasped directly by the senses, and yet which was not merely an abstract concept, could throw light upon the meaning of being or existence. Indeed, God, if he would exist, would fulfill the qualifications for existing transcendentally. And in this sense knowing something about God could tell us something about being. Unfortunately, however, what is known or understood about God is expressed (even when it would be revealed by God) in the language based upon being, that is, upon what does, in fact, exist.

Being can, however, be expressed in other words. And these "other words" for being have traditionally been called the *transcendentals:* one, true, good, and beautiful. Like being they are not able to be defined, strictly speaking. We may be able to say what a good car or a good man is, but be entirely unable to say what goodness is. Neither can the transcendentals be grasped directly by the senses. One can see that a statement is true; but this is not the same as seeing the truth of the statement. Nevertheless, because the transcendentals, like being, exist transcendentally, they would not differ fundamentally from being itself, at least so far as their mode of existing would be concerned. Thus are they able to operate as simply other words for being, telling us something more about being than what we already know. It is for this reason that one, true, good, and beautiful have been called the transcendental *properties* of being. They belong to being as something which is being's own (*propria*). And one of the ways in which it will be possible to determine the meaning "property" as applied to being, as well as the properties themselves, will be to ask whether one or the other of these properties of being add anything to being or not.

It was noted above that the question "What is being?" does not bear an answer, since being is not an essence; nor does being have an essence, even though it is true that every "a being" does have an essence. A similar situation will be met with the various transcendental properties of being as well. For example, if we attempt to ask "What is oneness?", "What is beauty?", etc., we cannot expect a definite or specifically meaningful answer to our question. The transcendentals exist transcendentally, as does being. This is why it will not be possible to understand them in some abstract fashion or give them a precise definition in accordance with genus and species. One cannot, for example, say exactly in what way a particular "a being" is good or exactly wherein its beauty may be said to consist. Neither can one sense goodness or beauty in a being in the same direct fashion that one can sense the quality of sweet or the shape and color of beauty. Like being, the transcendentals "climb beyond" (*transcendere*) individually existing things; though they are "beyond" the existing thing in the sense that they provide the basis and ground for that thing and for the qualities it possesses, as the absolutely necessary condition for the existence, and hence for the transcendental properties of existence, in a being. The goodness or the beauty of the individual "a being" does not exist somehow independently of the "a being" which is good or beautiful, any more than does its existence. One may recall the necessary dependence of being upon a being.

1. ONE

If we say that being or existence is one, we may mean nothing more than what Parmenides expressed in fragment 8 of his poem, that being is whole, unique, and complete as a well-rounded sphere, continuous and completely full (cf. Appendix I, Section 2). Being is one. Or one might think of oneness as a property of being in the way that Heraclitus does in fragment 50 when he states simply what "wisdom" says, namely that all things are one. They are all one in that each and every one of the things that does, in fact, exist has existence in common with all the other things that exist. They are all together in one vast well-rounded sphere. It would be in this sense that both Heraclitus and Parmenides say the same thing, namely that being or existence is one.

This approach, as we have seen earlier, is not entirely satisfactory. Although it is entirely true that all beings that exist have being or existence "in common," each "a being" has its own being or existence, not a common one. Each existent being does not participate or share in a larger "thing" called being. Existence is not something had in common like people participating in a social gathering or shareholders in a corporation; existence in each case, as we have seen, is limited by essence.

Taking the notion of one as a totality or as a whole, because it is made up of many parts, reveals the totally elastic meaning of the word. Thus we may speak of the United States as "one" nation. Leaving aside the question whether embassies in foreign lands are integral parts of the United States, it is clear that this is not the largest or the smallest "one" that we might speak of. The one nation is made up of fifty states, each of which is one; the states are made up of counties or similar subdivisions; the counties, of cities or towns, each of which is one. The cities are made up of sections or boroughs or suburbs, the sections of blocks, the blocks of houses, each of which is one. But there are also other "one's" in the house; one furnace, one washing machine; and this subdivision of "oneness" can be carried right down to the level of the atomic.

But just as there are "one's" that are very small, so there are "one's" which are very large. The one nation is part of one hemisphere, which is part of one world. The planet earth is in its turn part of one solar system, one galaxy, one universe. Clearly the notion of one is extremely elastic, so much so that it may appear totally meaningless in its vagueness. It can comprehend the complex simplicity of an atom or the vastness of the universe. It can be applied to the smallest and the largest, the simplest and the most complex of realities. All these are possible uses of the word one, indicating the basic ambiguity of its meaning. This ambiguity is, however, compounded.

a.   One as Unit

When we use the word one in relation to a being, or even to being, we may tend to confuse it with the Arabic numeral "1." To say that a being or a thing is one, in the sense that it is numercially "1" immediately throws the imagined oneness of any whole into question. For each of the parts of the whole would also be one; each can be enumerated or counted, and by the addition of these "one's" the number of the whole can be exactly ascertained.

To understand the sort of "one" that mathematics uses, it is necessary to understand the nature of enumeration. The one of mathematics is a one that counts and enumerates a multitude. It is a "unit" used for counting. Thus a large crowd of people, as, for example, at a political convention, may be said to constitute one multitude, or the representatives of one political party. But by counting or enumerating in units it is possible to "break up" that multitude into the number of unit members. In doing so we cease to treat the crowd on the convention hall floor as one crowd or a multitude, and begin considering it in terms of its member delegates as units. We make a head count of how many delegates are for which of the candidates. We thereby break up the crowd or multitude by counting in terms of the unit one.

Does this mean that the people comprising that multitude are really units? No. Units are what we use to count with, that is, what we use to "break up" multitudes. When we count, as mathematicians tell us, we make a one to one correspondence between the objects we are counting, for example, the number of people in the convention hall or the exact number supporting a particular candidate, and our series of counting numbers. The fact that there are 750 delegates attending the convention does not, however, mean that the number 750 somehow exists on the convention hall floor. Numbers are abstract symbols, and exist only in the mind; and counting is a strictly mental operation. The number one is simply the mathematical unit with which we begin counting. Thus in using mathematical units to break up a multitude, we are not counting units, we are using units to count with. It is true that the mathematician can count units— there are so many numbers in this class—but then he is no longer counting units but "objects," in the mathematical sense of that word. In any case, he is still using units to count with. Returning to the political scene, however, a convention delegate is not merely a unit to be counted, even though a prospective candidate may look at the delegate solely in this light. In other words, the relation between one and being is not the relation between the number "1" and "a being," as is signified in the operation of counting.

b.   One as Unity

What, then, does it mean to say that being is one? We have seen at least two different senses of the word "one" above. There is the one which is a whole or a totality, made up of many, and sometimes various, parts, a whole which we may number by means of another "one," namely the abstract number, the mathematical unit "1." There is, however, another meaning to the word one, a more specifically metaphysical meaning, which would be basis to these other meanings. This can be seen linguistically, for example, in the way that German or the Romance languages make no distinction between the number one and the indefinite article "a" or "an." Thus in German *ein,* or in French *un,* mean both the number one and the indefinite article. A being is *one* being. However, a being is numerically one being only because *a* being is a *being*.

Let us take an example. It is possible to treat a member delegate at the political convention as a *unit* vote to be counted only because the delegate is, in fact, a *unity*. He or she is one person: not one simply in a numerical sense, for each delegate has two arms, two legs, etc. Each member delegate is one in the sense that he or she has a wholeness, a completeness, an entirety which can in no wise be broken up without breaking the delegate up. Each one of the delegates is one being, and thus can he or she be counted by means of numerical units. We can count "one's" only if there are "a beings" that are one. Finally, with reference to the "one" of Parmenides and Heraclitus, it is possible to say that being or all things are one only because each and every a being is one being. For existence could be called one only because each and every individual "a being" does, in fact, exist. There is a danger in speaking of being or existence as one in this sense, that is, without indicating the necessary relation essence has to existence or being in a being. For it would tend to identify being and one, when, in fact, one is only a transcendental property of being. Being cannot be one in the sense that it represents the largest logical class of all classes. To define unity or oneness in this way would be to throw us right back into the ancient problematic of Parmenides and the hopelessly big (and vague) circle of being. Similarly, such a view of the one is not sufficiently fundamental; for being would be one only because each and every existing "a being" would be one being. To view being in this way would be to take a basically logical and mathematical position regarding being; and insofar as such a viewpoint would be essentially abstract and conceptual, it could only miss being.

c.   A Being Is One

As we have seen, existence is, in each and every case, limited by essence. Thus, as was suggested above, it is the meaning of being as one which is at the basis both of the naive metaphysics that "all things are one," as also at the basis of the mathematical "one." But what is meant by saying that something is one? If we saw this, do we merely mean that it is not "two?" What is the opposite of one? Is it many? Perhaps the opposite of one is other. Or is the opposite of one simply none? The opposite of one, at least in the metaphysical sense we are concerned with here, could not be other, since "other than one" would still be an-other one. Many, as more than one, would be an opposite of one in a mathematical sense; but we have seen that this sense is not sufficiently fundamental. To say that the opposite of one would be none or nothing may, at first sight, seem strange; however, we are here approaching its true meaning.

What is meant metaphysically by saying that something is one? When we speak of the oak tree as one, we mean, first, that its existence is divided from every other existence. It has an existence separate from other trees as things both within and without the forest, and even from other oak trees. The oak tree is one, as differentiated from the "others." Its existence is separate from that of other existing things, even of the same essential kind. Secondly, in saying that the oak tree is one we mean that its existence is undivided in itself. We mean that there is a wholeness, a completeness, and an entirety about the oak. It is "all one," all together, "all of a piece." This does not mean that parts cannot be distinguished in the oak tree; we can speak of leaves, branches, root system, etc.; but although parts can be distinguished, they can in no wise be cut off or separated without destroying the life of the tree as a whole. The oak tree is *one* being, that is, it is undivided in itself. There is a self-identical relation between this particular oak tree and its existence as an oak. Indeed, the oak may not be absolutely unique, that is, the only one of its kind (since there are, after all, other oaks besides this one); but there is only one "this particular oak," since this existence is limited by the essence oak to being this particular one. The oak outside my window is not just any old oak. Because of the characteristic of "oneness" or unity which goes along with being as one of its transcendental properties, this oak is a particular oak with an existence all its own. Its existence or being is one, and is its own. In fact, were the oak to lose this characteristic unity of its being, it would cease being the thing that it is. This is the sense in which it is correct to say that the opposite of one is none; for if the oak's being were to become divided in itself or to be absorbed somehow into other beings, in accordance with the All or None Law it would cease to be a being. This means that if the oak's being were to cease being one, it would cease being. And this is why oneness or unity is able to tell us something about being. Either a being has an existence that is one or it does not have being. This is why the oak will attempt to preserve its "unity" at all costs. It does this, of course, in the way oaks are prone to preserve their existences. It will draw nourishment from the soil, carbon dioxide from the air, and fight off the enemies of disease as best it can. For the oak to preserve its unity as a living and growing organism is to preserve its existence as an oak, given the reciprocal relation between being and a being, as it has been outlined above.

d.   Does Oneness Add to Being?

One way in which we may determine the meaning of saying that oneness is a transcendental property of being, as with the other transcendental properties of being as well, is to ask whether that property, in this case oneness, adds anything to being. Does saying that being or existence is one really add anything to what we already know about being? Clearly, we can add numerals: $1 + 1 = 2$. But it is equally clear that we cannot add apples. One apple cannot be added to another apple to get two apples. The coinherence of one apple into another is not, in fact, possible; unless, perhaps, we are interested in making apple sauce (seeds and all), in which case we are concerned with something other than individual apples. We cannot actually add apples, but only, in the mind, abstract numbers of apples taken as units. The being of a being is undivided in itself and divided off from every other being. This means that in saying that the existence or being of a being is a unity, all we are saying is that it is no more or no less than one. This means that oneness or unity does not add anything to being, except to deny division and assert separateness. The existence of a being cannot be more or less than one. A being cannot half-exist. This is simply the All or None Law: either a being has it (existence) or it does not.

It is in this sense that one is simply just another name for being. The fact that the being of a being is one does not in any way add anything to being, as though the being of a being could somehow be increased. It is, of course, true that *a* being may become more or less than what it is—a person can, for example, gain or lose weight. But it is not the person's existence that thereby gains or loses weight. We know, of course, that if a person gains or loses too much weight, his existence as a being may thereby be threatened. This occurs in virtue

of the necessary relation between being and a being, between a being and being. In saying that being is one, that it is undivided in
itself and divided off from every other being, we are merely express-
ing negatively what is meant by being positively. Thus, although
oneness does not add anything to being, it does add something to our
knowledge about being. Like the other transcendentals it provides a
richer insight into what it means to be.

e. The Determination of Oneness

The problem of determining exactly where the oneness or unity
of a particular being may lie is, of course, another matter. This pre-
sents little or no difficulty in the case of a being such as Ranger. Even
if Ranger should lose a leg in an accident, there may be less Ranger
there, but there is still no less existence or being. Ranger is still a being with the essence of dog limiting an existence which he either has
or does not have. But what of the "unity" of a rock, which may be
made up of many different elements and chemical compounds? What
is the unity here? One might say that when we have one atom of
iron, silicon, or some other mineral, then we have a unity of existence
limited by essence to being a certain kind of thing. Modern science,
however, indicates that there are also subatomic particles, electrons,
protons, neutrons, neutrinos, and numerous other subatomic particles
depending, to some extent, on how one wishes to count them. To
determine whether one can speak of unity at the level of the subatomic it would be necessary to decide whether one has something
which exists as a certain kind of thing. An electron or a neutron, for
example, would not seem to qualify on this score, since an electron
could be an electron of iron or one of carbon, and it is the same with
a neutron. Similarly the electron does not appear to have a self-
identical relation with itself; that is, it is not undivided in itself or
divided off from every other thing. Hence, below the level of the
atomic, at any rate, it does not seem possible to speak of something
as having identity; and this may, indeed, be one of the sources of
difficulty encountered by the nuclear physicist in trying to identify
different subatomic particles to determine where they are going and
what they are doing. They are not undivided in themselves, nor are
they clearly divided off from every other thing. And there would not

be a "certain kind of thing" that might thus be identified as such.

In all this it should, however, be recalled that we are primarily concerned not with the oneness of *a* being, but with oneness as a transcendental property of the *being* of a being. Hence, we can be sure that there is a unity to the existence of a molecule of water, for example, if only because it holds together, and resists attempts to separate it into its constituent elements of hydrogen and oxygen. This is indicated by the fact that a great deal of energy is required in order to break up this unity and reduce that molecule of water to free atoms of hydrogen and oxygen. The same is true of Ranger. He resists attempts to destroy his oneness; he resists division of himself and absorption into something or everything else. Nevertheless, oneness or unity is not primarily a property of Ranger, but a property of Ranger's being. Thus Ranger can lose a part of his ear in a fight with Fido, and not thereby lose a part of his existence. There is, because of the dependence of being on a being, however, a point beyond which Ranger will lose more than he can afford to lose, and continue in existence.

f.   Individuality and Individuation

As was seen above, metaphysics is a useless discipline. This does not, however, mean that application is not and cannot be made of notions that are fundamentally metaphysical. The relation between individual and society is, for example, a perennial problem in any and every human society. And no less significant, even for what may appear the most insignificant living or nonliving thing is its relation to other things that exist, because they may and do affect it in one way or another. Clearly, the meaning of individuality and individuation is always of paramount concern and importance, particularly for man. The question is: what light can our discussions on oneness or unity as a transcendental property of being throw upon this question?

As was seen, the being of a being is one. It is an "all or none" affair. Being cannot be partly had, partly not had. The only "thing" that the being of a being could change into would be non-being, which, as was suggested above, would represent a very peculiar sort of change. This does not mean that *a* being cannot and does not change. Still the being or existence of a being does not change, even though, as we have also seen, it is being or existence that represents the basis for such change, changes that can take place only within the limits of the essence of that particular being or thing.

The being or existence of a being, then, remains one; existence or being is limited by essence to being this particular "a being." To say that being is one thus means that being, because of the existence-limiting function of essence is undivided in itself and divided off from every other being. Since this is the case, one might wonder whether an absolute or isolated individualism would not be the only possible metaphysics, a sort of metaphysics of the unique. There is, indeed, one side to the meaning of "one" which would seem to lend support to this view, namely the fact that being one means being undivided in itself, that is, being whole, complete, and entire. However, there is also another side to the meaning of "one," namely the fact that being one means being divided off from others. In other words, there can be no oneness or individuality unless there are others. This fact would tend to undercut even the possibility, let alone the viability, of an absolute or isolated individualism. It would also tend to throw into question a solipsism which attempted to speak only in terms of one mind and the states thereof. There is no "one," in the sense that it is divided off from others, unless there are, in fact, other one's as well. To be one implies that there must be an-other one.

But just as others are necessary for the very meaning of individuality, so also are they necessary for individuation. The self, or the particular or individual thing, is defined and achieves whatever identity it may have in terms of other things and other selves. No self or thing, so long as we have the kind of world that we do, can individuate itself totally by itself and independently of any of the other things that may exist. The particular thing becomes the being that it is, at least in part, through the effect and influence, or the reaction thereto, which other things have upon it. This does not mean that the individual thing is simply the result of those things that influence it or to which it reacts, as though a self, for example, were merely the sum total of its affects. If this were the case, then the individual existence could not remain undivided in itself. One could not speak of "one existence," since it would merely be the result of the divided pieces of so many other existences. Further, each and every thing that exists is also a certain kind of being, and this means that the changes that operate in that "a being" take place within a certain limit. These changes cannot merely be those that result or are forced from outside without destroying that one limited "a being" which must be and remain undivided and self-identical with itself. Thus the human self, for example, cannot be merely the product or the result of its environment. There is a "certain kind of being" involved here, in this case a human being that is free to choose, or at least to accept or reject. Such a freedom could clearly not be absolute, for reasons we have also seen. There is one individual divided off from others only if there are actually others; and it is in terms of these others alone that individuality would have meaning and individuation would take place.

g. Summary

In this section we have been concerned with the meaning of the first of the transcendental properties of being, namely one. It may not be understood in the sense of the mathematical numeral of the same name. There is a difference between a unit and a unity. And the one of metaphysics is the one of a unity. Units are what we use to count with, that is to break up multitudes. We are able to add units; we are not able to add unities without destroying them. Nor can the one of metaphysics be the One of Heraclitus or Parmenides, as containing all the "one's" that exist, simply because they exist. As we have seen, being is not something which beings or things share in common; each "a being" has its own. Nor may being or existence be understood as the largest of all logical classes.

We attempted to delineate the meaning of one as the transcendental property of the being of a being through the question whether one adds to being, arguing that what is one is divided off from every other thing and is undivided in itself. Oneness or unity is something which the being of a being either has or does not have; it is not something which adds anything to being. A being cannot exist partly, half-exist, so to speak. In accordance with the All or None Law, either it is or it is not. The problem of the actual determination of "one existence" first in physical reality, and then in social reality was considered. It was argued that we cannot speak of identity below the level of the atomic. And in the section on individuality and individuation the light which the discussion on one as a transcendental property of being can throw on the relation between individual and society was presented in outline form. It was seen that the individual requires a society to be an individual, since to be divided from others requires that there be others. In the case of the human self, however, the element of self-determination must also be present, that is if human being would genuinely be undivided in itself.

bibliography

Allers, Rudolf. "Ens et Unum Convertuntur," *Philosophical Studies in Honor of Ignatius Smith*, ed. J. K. Ryan. Westminster, Md.: Newman, 1952, pp. 65–75. The article is in English.

Aristotle. *Metaphysics*, III, 4; IV, 2; V, 7–8; X, 1–3, 6. Bradley, F. H. *Appearance and Reality*. 2 ed.; Oxford: Clarendon Press, 1897, ch. VIII: "Things."

James, William. *Pragmatism and Other Essays*. New York: Meridian Books, 1955, Lecture IV: "The One and the Many."

Maritain, Jacques. *Preface to Metaphysics*. New York: Sheed, 1939, pp. 91–97.

Pegis, Anton. "The Dilemma of Being and Unity," *Essays in Thomism*, ed. R. E. Brennan. New York: Sheed, 1942, pp. 151–183.

Plato. *Parmenides* 127–135.

Salmon, E. G. "Metaphysics and Unity," *Progress in Philosophy*. Milwaukee: Bruce, 1955, pp. 47–60.

2.   TRUE

The English word "true" means something solid and firm. According to philologists it is, with the German word *treu*, related to the Indogermanic word for tree. Hence, true is what is solid and firm. As an extension of this meaning, "to be true" means to be characterized by good faith; thus we speak of a true friend, in the sense of someone who is faithful and loyal. We also speak of a statement as true; we speak of things as true to a standard or rule, "true to the mark."

The Greek word for truth has a slightly different sense. It means the full and real state of affairs; it is that which does not deceive us into believing what it is not. The Greek word for true is *alēthēs*, that is, what is unconcealed, unhidden, and undeceptive, literally *a* (not) and *lēthō* (to escape notice). The true is what is real, as it is revealed in its disclosure; hence, that which does not escape notice. The Greeks, as can clearly be seen both in Plato and Aristotle for example, *identified* the real and the true. Thus Aristotle can say, "Truth is to say what is, is; what is not, is not." (*Meta.* IV 7, 1011b 25). We find an identification similar to the one made by the Greeks in our own language when we speak of "real" or "true" lace, "real" or "true" gold, as distinguished from "false gold" or iron pyrites. For the Greek to say that the real is true, and the true real, was entirely self evident. The word for real (*on*) could also mean true; and the word for true (*alēthēs*), real. Truth was not merely a transcendental property of being, but identical with it.

a. The True and the Real

If one simply takes the Greek view of truth in its ungarnished form, then "getting into contact with truth" would be the same as getting into contact with being. In other words, if truth is identical with being, then it would appear to be merely a question of making the being which exists disclose the secrets of its truth (that is, its being). For if the true and the real are identical, and if a being is accounted real, then it is merely a question of somehow ferreting the truth of being out of the "a being." Thus if we want the "truth" about the piece of chalk, for example, then it is a question of "getting into" that piece of chalk in such a way that its truth becomes apparent, or a question of somehow forcing the truth out of the piece of chalk. Since it does not seem possible somehow to get inside the piece of chalk, the best means gaining the truth about the piece of chalk would appear to be forcing the truth out of the piece of chalk by tearing the "a being" open or grinding it up.

This is not to suggest that the efforts of the nuclear physicist to discover the secrets of the atom by breaking it open will not assist

toward scientific truth. However, it is not tearing the being open
that is productive of scientific truth, but the formulation and recon-
struction by the scientist of what must, in fact, have occurred which
gives the nuclear physicist glimpses about the truth of sub-atomic
reality. Truth is not somehow hidden in a being, so that it might be
ferreted out of its hiding place by some means or another, any more
than can the being of a being be localized exactly in the "a being,"
and thus be ferreted out. Certainly it is impossible to discover the
being of something, or its truth for that matter, by destroying it.
There are two reasons why this cannot be the case. Firstly, being
does not exist in a being in that way that the particular "a being"
exists, as we have seen; being is not in a being the way the heart, for
example, is in the human body. Being exists transcendentally, and so,
presumably, would truth as a transcendental property of being. Secondly, truth is not the property of *a* being, in such a way that it
might be found somewhere inside the existing "a being"; truth is a
transcendental property of being. Thus we may properly speak of
white as a property of Ranger, but true would not be a property of
Ranger, but of Ranger's being. We may, of course, speak of Ranger
as "true"; but we then mean something else: we mean that he is faithful and loyal. In other words, we are speaking about a property of
Ranger, not about a property of Ranger's being.

b.   The Truth of Statements

Truth cannot be identified with a being, nor simply with being.
Truth is not identical with being, but a property of it; and true is not
even a property of a being. True and real cannot be identified if only
because truth is also found elsewhere. For example, when I say
"Felix is a black cat," I say something I know to be true. Truth is not
simply "in being"; it is also in my mind, and can be attached to propositions and statements which are made about beings by virtue of
the mind.

But although truth can be in the mind and attached to propositions, this does not mean that truth has lost all connection with being; for what is known to be true by the mind is known by an existing mind, something that is also "in being." Hence, whatever is
known must in some way exist, if only as a state of the mind that

knows it. Nevertheless, truth cannot be said to exist solely and simply in the mind. For one thing, truth is a transcendental property of the existence of a being, and this existence, and hence the truth which would be its property, is the absolutely necessary condition for the "a being." Even the dependence of truth upon the mind, as "in being," must rest upon the mind of a being that does exist, and hence is also in being. Further, one may ask about the source for the truth of the statement that Felix is a black cat. It is not possible to find this truth in the proposition itself, as though it were contained, by some sort of magic, in the copulative verb "is" which joins the subject "Felix" with the predicated "black cat." As we have seen, it is possible to use the verb "is" in a proposition such as "A leprechaun is an Irish dwarf" without in any way connoting existence. The two terms "Felix" and "black cat," as joined in a proposition would make the statement true or false only if Felix actually does exist, and if she is, in fact, a black cat. In other words, it is indeed true to say that there is truth in the mind. It may even be true to say that there is no truth independent of a knowing mind which knows something to be true. Nonetheless, there are at least two facts which must temper this conclusion: there is, first of all, the factor of existence or being which may or may not be known to be true; and secondly, there is the fact of error. Let us take the factor of existence first.

That truth is not simply in the mind can be seen from the fact that something can be true, and yet not be known by the mind. The identification of what is known by the mind with what is true cannot be made. For example, I may think it is true that there are no man-eating sharks in the waters where I am swimming. But no matter how much I may be convinced of the "truth" that there is no danger from sharks, this does not mean that my conviction, however firm, is necessarily true. There is, besides the truth of personal conviction or of statements, the truth which is a genuine property of the being of a being, independent of what I may be convinced or state to be true. There is, after all, error.

c.   The Fact of Error

The fact of error cannot, unfortunately, be ignored in any consideration of truth, nor can its influence be considered negligible. There is such a thing as "false knowledge" or error; and this indicates further that truth cannot be identified with what the mind knows, or believes to be true. One may, of course, say that false knowledge is not knowledge, that there is only true knowledge, or it cannot be called knowledge. The fact remains, however, that knowledge which may, in fact, be false necessarily involves elements which are true. Thus if I am a member of the Flat Earth Society, and insist that the earth is flat—because if it were not, then all the carts in creation would roll away—there are elements of truth in that false knowledge. For example, there is an earth, and it does appear to be flat. In other words, there are pieces of true knowledge involved in the false knowledge that I may claim about the shape of the planet.

This fact of error or false knowledge indicates three very important things about truth. In the first place, the fact of error necessarily implies truth, at least some elements of truth. For one can discover that an error has been made only if that error could be seen in relation to something that is true. The statement of pre-Copernican man that "The sun revolves about the earth" can be discovered to be an error only if the statement that the earth revolves around the sun can be shown to be the true, or at least be shown to be the simpler and more convincing hypothesis. There is error only if there is a truth with which to correct that error. But the fact of error indicates first that truth is not simply in the mind, since the "truth" that the earth is flat could be discovered and corrected only by the discovery of the truth that the earth is, in fact, round. The fact of error indicates that truth cannot *simply* be in the mind.

The fact of error indicates something even more important. There is no error unless there is a mind. There is, for example, no error in being. There is *really* no such thing as "false gold," only *true* iron pyrites. There is *really* no such things as a false or counterfeit van Gogh, only a true imitation. There is error only where there is a mind capable of making errors, in the same way that a mind is required in order to discover the falsity of its errors by means of a truth which corrects that error. There is no error or falsity in reality. This fact has yet another important consequence. It means, for example, that truth implies a necessary relation to the mind. Truth is not simply "in being," somehow to be ferreted out. Truth is also in the mind as that which corrects the errors that are made by the mind. But because of the fact that truth is not simply in the mind, since the truth that corrects error is not, at least at the time that the error is made, simply in the mind, the fact of error means that truth is also "in being," and not merely in the being of the mind, if one may so speak.

d. Truth as Relation

From the fact that truth is not simply in the mind, but also in being, such that error (which is only in the mind) might be corrected by truth; and from the fact that truth is not simply in being, but necessarily related to the mind, so that error might indeed get corrected, philosophers in the West have generally tended to view truth as essentially the relation between thing and mind. This is the famous adage: *veritas est adaequatio rei et intellectus,* truth is the agreement of the thing and the intellect. The unfortunate aspect of this "definition" of truth is that it speaks of an agreement between thing and mind. For since to agree is to agree with someone or something, the question arises in the case of the agreement between thing and mind: who agrees with whom? Does the mind agree with the thing (*veritas est adequatio intellectus ad rem*)? This has been characterized as the ancient and mediaeval view of truth. Or does the thing agree with the mind (*veritas est adaequatio rei ad intellectum*)? The latter formulation of the adage is said to be that of Kant and of the majority of modern and contemporary philosophers after Kant. Such an interpretation of the adage states simply that in order for the thing to be known by the knowing mind that thing must agree, that is, be made to accord with the mind's modes of knowledge; otherwise it cannot be known.

(i) The Relation of Mind to Thing

To decide between these very different views of the truth relation is no easy matter. In favor of what has been characterized as the ancient and mediaeval view of truth is the fact that if we ask, as we asked in the case of the one, whether truth adds anything to being, we find something curious. Clearly, the fact that I know that Ranger exists adds nothing to the being or existence of Ranger; nor does it subtract anything from Ranger if I know his existence, or, so far as one can tell, if I fail to know that he exists. One may, of course, say that in knowing Ranger this particular dog comes to take up a new existence, or an existence of a different sort, in my mind. However, this "new" existence is clearly not identical with Ranger's own existence; and nothing is either added or subtracted from Ranger's actual existence, whether he is known or not. A situation analogous to this might be that of the teacher who does not necessarily lose any of the knowledge he possesses in passing it on to his students: if anything, he comes to understand it better. By the same token, if Ranger were to gain or lose something by being known (or by not being known), then the more people or other beings that knew Ranger would take more and more from his existence or add more and more to it, until Ranger would either be overburdened with his own fame, or else a marvelous new method for reducing would have been discovered, of all things, by a metaphysician. One would merely strive to be known by as many people as possible, since this would subtract more and more from one's existence. This would obviously be absurd, and there are good metaphysical reasons why it is. The fact that I know that Tom is overweight does not add anything to Tom, either to his essence or to his existence; nor, unfortunately, does it subtract anything either. Tom still exists as he is and as what he is, whether I know this or not.

But although knowing that Tom exists or that Tom is overweight in no way adds or subtracts from Tom's essence or existence, it does add something to my being, that is, to the being of the knower. I am a different person for having known Tom. Truth, then, does add to being. It does not add anything to that which is known, but to the one that knows. From this one might argue that it is only because the mind accords with the thing that the relation of truth between mind and thing can be established, and something be added to the knower. For it would seem that since the mind adds nothing to the "a being" (or subtracts nothing from it) in knowing it, then it is the mind which is the passive recipient of that which, with truth, is added to it. Truth is, then, the agreement or accord of the mind with the thing. Only this would make such addition possible.

(ii) The Relation of Thing to Mind

The above view of truth would be entirely adequate if it were not for the fact of error. For error or false knowledge could be added to the knower in the same simple way that truth would be; and it would be extremely doubtful that the "addition" of error could be considered as really adding something to the knower, certainly in the positive sense that is normally understood as knowledge. In fact, such an "addition" could prove highly perilous to the knower, as, for example, when I make the error of believing that there are no sharks in shark-infested waters. But since there is no error or falsity in reality, but only with a mind, then this means that the mind is never simply a passive recipient, simply absorbing and soaking in truth like a sponge, adding to itself because the mind is constantly agreeing or according itself with the thing. The fact of error indicates that the mind is not inactive. It is no mere receiver or passive recipient. It is fundamentally active in the activity of knowing because it knows.

The mind can, however, also discover that its errors are, in fact, errors, only if it has a truth to correct such errors. The fact that the mind makes errors, or is able to correct its own errors, tells us something about truth, as well as about the mind. First, it tells us that truth is what we use to correct error with. Secondly, it tells us that the mind is fundamentally active. In other words, truth is not the result of a slavish conformity of the mind to the thing. The kind of addition which truth adds to my being is an addition which *I* add to the being that I am. In knowing the mind does, and must, work.

The fact that truth represents an addition to the knower means that the knower can know only what he *can* know. At first sight, this may appear trivial. But however insignificant it may appear, it has the greatest possible importance for human knowledge. It means that what would be known, that is, what would be added to the knower, must be able to be known. It must be know-able. This means, *first* of all, that it must be able to be known *by me*. I must be prepared to know it, to meet it, since I could receive only what I am prepared to receive. This is the truth contained in the post-Kantian view of truth as the agreement of the thing to my mind. If the thing does not conform to my modes of knowledge, it is not something which *I* am able to know. The mind must be active if errors are to be corrected. It must also be active if new things are to be known, that is, if mental growth is actually to take place. If new truth is, in fact, to be added to my being, the things which must conform to the modes of the mind's knowing could only be received by modes which were constantly adapting to the new things that must be known.

For the thing to be knowable, it is not merely a question of its according with the mind's modes of knowing, as though what is known depended for its creation as something known solely upon the knowing mind. For the thing to be able to be known, for it to serve the mind in the correction of error, the thing must exist as what it is. That which is to be known must be knowable. It must be able to be known for the fact *that* that is, and as *what* it is. This would also be required for the thing to be able to add to the knower. The mind, indeed, corrects its own errors. But the truth which we use to correct error with cannot be wholly dependent upon the mind. The mind does not live disembodied in some splendid isolation. If it did, the mind could not even correct its own errors. In other words, for the thing to be known by the mind, the thing must, indeed, agree and accord with the mind that knows it. The mind is and must be active in the correction of its own error, just as it was, in fact, active in making the error in the first place. But for that correction to take place the mind also requires the thing and its being.

e.   Does Truth Add to Being?

Truth represents an addition; not to that which is known, but to the knower. There is a process of coming to know which is not merely a passive receptivity, but an active process engaged in by the mind. That the mind is active can be seen from the fact of error; that the mind works and is operative in the process of human knowing can also be seen from the fact that it corrects its own errors. But although the mind is essentially active, truth nevertheless represents an addition. The character of this addition must, however, be carefully understood and delineated.

One might compare the process of human knowing with that of assimilation. Francis Bacon suggests this comparison in his essay *Of Studies*, when he says: "Some books are to be tasted, others to be swallowed, and some few to be chewed and digested." He uses the metaphor of the assimilation of nourishment to approach the truth value to be found in different materials for study. Thus one may compare the taking in of the truth contained in books, or in anything for that matter to the intake of good. When food is taken into the physical organism, the vitamins and minerals which are thus ingested get made over and transformed through various biochemical processes into the cells, tissue, and bone necessary for the growth and development of the organism. In any process of assimilation there is something like, and yet unlike, the physical organism which is ingested and transformed; it is assimilated (*ad-similare*, made similar to) the organism itself, so that it becomes the very stuff of it.

In the process of knowing there is likewise something that is both like and unlike the mind. The turnip or the piece of chalk is unlike the mind; we cannot somehow bring the piece of chalk, whole and entire, into our mind, any more than the turnip we eat can be substituted directly for worn out cells and tissues; the muscle tissue in one's arm is not replaced by whole turnips. Yet, there is something similar both to mind and thing such that the thing can be assimilated by the mind. For example, both exist. It is only because the thing exists that it can be added to the mind in a process similar to that of assimilation. This is the only way in which the mind is able to get "inside" something. The nuclear physicist can get inside the workings of the atom only by getting everything that is to be known about the atom inside his mind. To do this, what is unlike must somehow be made like the mind.

At this point one might mention Bergson's method of "getting with" the flow of existence by means of an intuition which would also be temporally oriented toward such a flow of being. However, it is possible to "get with" being only by getting being somehow within me. It is not possible to get inside the piece of chalk to grasp its truth. This is not the way truth is "in being."

But although there are similarities between the assimilation of nourishment and that of truth, there are also fundamental differences. Thus, for example, when one assimilates too much physical nourishment into the system, he tends to gain weight. Whereas when one assimilates knowledge, and thereby adds something to himself, he does not increase physically, or even metaphysically, for that matter. The more truth added to one's being does not increase the metaphysical size, so to speak, of the "a being's" existence. As was seen earlier, one cannot exist more or less, in the way that one's weight can be more or less. One's existence does not change, even though it is the basis for change in a being that changes. Thus the kind of assimilation involved in taking in nourishment and in the addition of truth is different. In the case of physical nourishment something physical is added to a being; Felix grows larger the more fish she is fed. The assimilation of knowledge does not mean that one's existence or mind grows or gets bigger. Added knowledge may, of course, swell one's head, but this is something different.

The reason for the difference between these two kinds of assimilation should be clearer. When Felix assimilates the piece of raw fish, the being that is the piece of fish is destroyed and becomes bone and tissue for Felix. When the mind knows, on the other hand, the existence of that which is known is in no way affected, unless, of course, one intends to do something with that knowledge. The fact that I experience the armadillo in no way changes the armadillo. It changes me. Truth is added to me. But, as we have seen, truth is not merely added to my being as though I were merely a passive recipient. It is *I* that add truth to the being that I am; however, the being of that "a being" that I am is and remains the same. Hence, I am changed, and yet unchanged, by the addition of truth. I am unchanged in that my existence, as limited by the essence that I have, remains the same existence I had before. Yet I am changed in the sense that what was error or ignorance before has been replaced by truth; and it is I who have corrected my own error and dispelled my own ignorance.

Clearly the "addition" of truth is an addition of a peculiar sort. The assimilation of knowledge is not simply the reception of something which enlarges my existence, much less my physical size. For it is I who act to make the thing conform to my modes of knowledge; it is I who correct the error and dispel the ignorance that is my own. Truth is an addition to my being which I myself must make. But since I am the one who makes it, I remain essentially the same "I"; and the existence which is mind remains the same existence, one limited to this specific instance, by the essence man. This would mean that no matter how much I might come to know, I cannot become a god; and no matter how little I may know, or how ignorant or how much in error I may be, I cannot become a brute animal.

The "addition" of truth is also a peculiar one in the sense that no subtraction is possible. The dispensing of knowledge to others through the communication of our thoughts and ideas in no way subtracts from the knowledge we already possess. If anything such continued communication tends to reinforce that knowledge, as one soon discovers in attempting to argue against oft repeated and commonly accepted opinions. This is why parents need not fear the demythologizing of the idea of Santa Claus in the young. Literally nothing is thereby really subtracted, for nothing had really been added in the first place, even in the peculiar sense of the addition of truth. What was really ignorance or error is corrected by the truth that it is really the parents who are Santa Claus. One may grieve at the loss ("subtraction") of the beauty of the child's image of Santa Claus, but one might also argue that the truth which replaces it is far better. And in any case, there is a stage in life beyond which belief in Santa Claus becomes a little out of place.

Clearly, the kind of "addition" and "subtraction" characteristic of truth and its relation to the mind can be properly gauged only when the kind of existence that ideas, concepts, images, etc., have in the mind has been considered. To this question we must now turn.

f. The Existence of Ideas

What kind of existence do ideas or concepts have? This question normally comes up again in any treatment of metaphysics. It arose, for example, when we considered being as a concept, and when we inquired whether being could be know conceptually. There are all sorts of things in the mind: ideas, concepts, images, memories, fictions, etc. What is the status of all these ideas in the light of what we have seen above about truth? For example, we have in our mind the concept "dog," which is independent of any actually existing dog, since we would still have the concept even if all the dogs in existence should suddenly cease to exist. Similarly, we can have in our mind the image or idea of one of the hounds of the Baskervilles, as something entirely fictional. Or we can have the idea of Fido, as a dog actually existing before us. What kind of existence do these various "ideas" have?

One problem with the existence status of ideas in the mind is their very changeable character; they seem to be constantly coming into and going out of existence. Thus I may think of Shakespeare's character Hamlet; but when I stop thinking of him, the idea of Hamlet ceases to exist. It may be true that the literary embodiment of the character Hamlet in the play of the same name may exist in written characters of the English language in many different texts and copies; nevertheless, Hamlet "exists" only when he is read or produced dramatically. The idea of Hamlet depends for its existence upon the existence of those who read or think about the play created by Shakespeare. This dependence of the existence of certain ideas upon the existence of some mind can be seen in the way that an original idea, for example, the secret for Roman mortar, the formula for a new product, or a recipe for a particular dish may "die" with the originator. The idea depends so much for its existence upon the existence of its originator that when he ceases to exist the secret formula or original idea dies with him.

The existence of the idea of Fido, in mine or another's mind, does not depend for its existence quite to the same extent upon mine or another's existence, as does the secret formula or the original idea for example. The idea, in the sense of the image, of Fido will exist in my mind so long as Fido continues to appear before me and I turn my head in the right direction. The idea or image of Fido, that is, if it would truly be an idea or image of Fido, depends more upon the existence of Fido than it does upon my own or upon another's existence. In other words, the idea of Fido is much less dependent upon my existence than it is the idea of hounds of the Baskervilles, and much more upon the actually existing dog before me. Indeed, the idea of Shakespeare's Hamlet does not depend entirely upon my existence, but to a great extent upon the play written by Shakespeare. In fact, even the most original idea, for example, the idea for the play *Hamlet* in the mind of its author depended upon things which actually existed, for example, Hollingshead's *Chronicles* and Shakespeare's experiences of men and different situations. The dependence of ideas, whether upon my own existence or upon that of existing things, is, then, a relative, never an absolute dependence. This would be in line with what we have seen concerning the meaning of truth as relation. Nothing known can be totally independent of what actually exists. On the other hand, nothing that exists *as known* can, obviously, be independent of the knower. The existence of ideas in our mind, then, introduces the question of the relative degree of dependence of ideas upon my own existence, upon the existence of the things that are, in fact, known, and even upon the existence of another person upon whom I depend for information about a particular matter.

But if the existence status of the ideas in our mind depends in a relative way upon my own and upon the existence of other things and other persons, then how is this degree of dependency to be determined? In the case of the individual idea this may not be an easy matter, given the admittedly complex interdependencies involved. But there is a way, at least theoretically, to determine the degrees of dependency for the ideas we have in our mind in terms of what we have seen above. As was noted earlier, the mind is and must be active, as can be seen from the fact of error and the necessary correction of errors which are the mind's own. The mind is clearly more active in the cases in which the existence of the idea in my mind depends more upon my mind than upon someone or something else. Shakespeare's creation of the play and the character of Hamlet required a great deal of mental activity, much more than the activity required of one who merely reads the play or watches it performed. On the other hand, the mental activity required for knowing the white Samoyede, which stands in front of me, requires much less activity on my part. It is true that the mind is never totally inactive or purely receptive even in this latter case, as we have seen; nevertheless, the mind is not forced to work so hard in recognizing the white dog that the dependency for the existence of that idea might be said to rest more upon the mind than upon the thing.

It must, of course, be noted that the dependencies can be highly complex. The memory of the last school mascot, a German shepherd also called Ranger, depends upon a memory image; and yet because the existence of that idea depends upon *my* memory, it would appear to depend more upon my existence than upon that of the former mascot, particularly since he no longer exists. Similarly, the idea of a manned rocket ship to Mars has a complex set of dependencies related both to the planet itself, or better, to what is known about it, and the plans and projects in the minds of the scientific and engineering community working for the realization of the project. Even over a period of time the existence status of such ideas would seem to change, in accordance with their relative dependencies. In its initial stages the manned rocket ship might be no more than a dream, the fancy of a visionary; but as knowledge and the instruments necessary for the realization of the idea become more viable, the idea comes to depend more and more upon the existing things involved. In fact, this is exactly why the project becomes more and more viable or feasible. The key to these various relative dependencies of ideas remains, however, the extent to which the mind is active, and thus the extent to which the ideas about what does, did, or will exist depend upon the existence of the knower or the things known.

What exactly does this mean? It means that the relative dependence of mind upon thing and thing upon mind, and hence the "relative existential weight" of various ideas can be gauged, at least theoretically, by determining the extent to which the mind is itself active in the project. This is why original thought and work is so difficult. To bring about the realization of what does not yet, in fact, exist requires the mind to be extremely active in the correction of its own errors and the overcoming of its own ignorance.

g. Education and Learning

Although metaphysics is essentially useless, it is not, as we have seen without applications and implications. For this reason it might be well to draw out some of the implications of the view of truth that has been outlined above in its relation to a theory of learning or education. It should come as no surprise that a theory of truth, and a general overview of the way in which we know, should have serious and important implications on what is commonly termed learning theory; and obviously learning theory has a great deal to do with education.

If the mind is fundamentally active in the process of knowing, and if it is necessarily active in the correction of error and the dispelling of ignorance, then this means that the learning or gaining of truth cannot be merely a matter of receiving or absorbing vast amounts of data, facts, and information. Such "forced feeding" may be necessary at the introductory levels of a particular science or discipline. But it is not yet education. The mind is not a large box or an artfully designed memory bank in which data and information may be stored and from which it may be retrieved. Nor is the mind a sponge. For although the student may pick up a great deal by a process similar to osmosis, the mind does not thereby gain truth. Facts do not correct ignorance and error. The mere absorption of data may introduce a great amount of information into the mind, but it can also introduce a great deal of ignorance and error, without that development of the critical faculties which would enable the student to tell the difference.

Since the ignorance and error are the student's own, it is the student who must do the correcting. The teacher cannot do it for him. If learning implies mental growth, the teacher can no more grow for the student than parents can do the physical growing for their children. The teacher cannot learn for his students; he cannot even teach them. The most he can do is to show them how to learn by learning, and continuing to learn, along with the student. To become a chemist or a sociologist the student must learn to think as a chemist or sociologist does. The teacher can set the example on this score, showing the student how a chemist or a sociologist thinks and works. This is why it is important, if not essential, that the teacher be what he is teaching. For the teacher of sociology can give a continuing example of one thinking within the field of sociology only if he continues to think and work as a sociologist; and he can do this only if he continues to learn more and more about what he teaches.

In the final analysis, however, it is the student who must learn to think chemistry or to think sociology. There are, of course, means of motivating the student, when the personal incentive to learn may not be present. These means are essentially the same in every age of educational history, namely the carrot and the whip. Indeed, in each age the carrot and the whip will be different, but there are always carrots to draw the student forward and whips to urge him on from behind. The old adage, corny though it may sound, remains true: the horse can be led to water, but cannot be made to drink. Every educator, in the end, will admit that external modes of motivation are unsuccessful. The teacher cannot force learning on the student. The teacher can force the student to do his own learning only by forcing him to think, that is, by making him aware of his own ignorance, gently of course, and thus forcing him to correct his own errors. This method of education is as old as Socrates. And in the final analysis the basic method of education has not changed radically, because man has not essentially changed. There is still ignorance and error, and since the ignorance and error is the student's, it is still the student who must dispel his own ignorance and correct his own errors. In so doing his mind is forced to become active, and to become actively engaged in his own education.

The teacher cannot reveal ignorance and error simply by stating what the student believes to be true is false, much less by simply stating dogmatically that the student knows nothing. Parmenides made the same point toward the end of the prologue to his poem (cf. Appendix I, Section 1): to know all things it is not sufficient simply to know what is true and what is false; one must also be able to know and to explain why the false is false. The same effect can be achieved by indicating to the student certain facts that he may have overlooked, by pointing out where a line of reasoning is incorrect, or by showing that certain assumptions and presuppositions have been made of which the student may have been unaware, and indicating their implications or consequences. This latter can be particularly effective, since it is precisely at this point that ignorance and error can be best shown up, namely at their roots. Generally one is not fully aware of the assumptions that he actually makes, or the presuppositions that he or his culture, or his subculture, simply takes for granted. They are, after all, taken for granted; which means that generally they are not examined for what they are, nor are their full ramifications considered.

h. Summary

Linguistically, true means, in English, what is solid and firm; in Greek, what is unhidden and does not escape notice. The Greek identification of true and real cannot, however, be retained, since it is not possible to get the true out of the real or the real out of the true. The true is not in "a being," nor is it "in" the being of a being in such a fashion. Truth is a property of the being of a being, not of a being. It is also the property of statements, but only because there would be a being having existence or being (and a mind) capable of making such statements. Truth is not, however, simply in statements or in the mind. There is, for example, the fact of error, which indicates that truth is not simply in the mind. The fact that truth is also in being as well as in the mind suggested the possibility that truth is but the relation between thing and mind. But in which direction is this relation? Must the mind conform to the thing, or the thing to the mind? The view that the mind must conform to the thing is supported by the fact that truth adds something to the mind, but not to the thing. Unfortunately, there is again the factor of error. For here "addition," or the "subtraction" which might occur through the correction of the error, would take on a curious meaning. But if the mind must be fundamentally active in knowing and in the correction of error, then it would appear that the thing necessarily conforming itself to the mind and its modes of knowing would be the more likely view of truth. In other words, for something to be known it must be knowable: it must be able to be known by the knower, and it must exist and be what it is in order to be able to be known. Truth, then, is being as knowable. But truth is also that which is able to correct error for the knower, an error and an ignorance which is the knower's own to correct.

The way in which truth is added to the knower was compared to the way in which an organism assimilates nourishment. This addition of truth does not, however, add to the being or existence of a being, nor does it enlarge the "a being" itself, at least in physical dimensions. The "change" which knowledge introduces into a being can take place only within the limits of the essence of that "a being" and on the basis of its existence. It is this basis of existence which offers an approach to the meaning or existence status of various kinds of ideas, and their relative dependence upon the mind or upon the thing. This problem of the relative dependence of ideas was solved, at least theoretically, by appealing to that which is most actively engaged in the actual knowing of what is known. Thus original ideas depend almost entirely upon the knowing mind for their existence, since the mind must do the most work; whereas the reception of a sense image may require very little activity on the part of the mind. This view of truth and of the existence status of our ideas leads to a particular view of learning theory, and hence of education, indicating that the positions taken in metaphysics are not without consequence in other extremely important areas of human endeavor.

exercises

1. Why consider the so-called transcendentals? What is a transcendental?
2. Compare one as unit and one as unity.
3. To say that everything is one is ambiguous. Why?
4. What does it mean to say that being is one?
5. Does oneness add to being?
6. Discuss the applicability of the All or None Law.
7. Oneness is a property of being, not of a being. Discuss and exemplify.
8. Discuss the case for the "isolated individual," in relation to the meaning of oneness.
9. Are the linguistic uses of the word "true" of any assistance in understanding truth as a transcendental property of being?

10. Why is it not possible to identify the true and the real?
11. Truth is simply in the mind. Discuss.
12. What does the fact of error tell us?
13. If truth implies both mind and thing, then it consists in the relation between the two. Discuss the possibilities here.
14. Does truth add to being? How does this relate to the view of truth as conformity of mind to thing?
15. What light does the fact that the mind is active throw upon the nature of the truth relation?
16. Compare the assimilation of nourishment with the "addition" of truth.
17. Discuss the existence status of our various ideas. How might this status be grounded?
18. What are the implications of the view of truth taken here for a theory of learning or education?

bibliography

Aquinas, Thomas. *Truth,* tr. R. W. Mulligan. Chicago: Regnery, 1952, vol. I, question I: "Truth" and question III: "Ideas."

Aristotle. *Metaphysics* IV, 7–8; IX, 10.

Bergson, Henri. *An Introduction to Metaphysics,* tr. T. E. Hulme. 2 ed.; New York: Liberal Arts, 1955.

Berkeley, George. *A Treatise Concerning the Principles of Human Knowledge,* ed. C. M. Turbayne. New York: Liberal Arts, 1957, pt. 1.

Bradley, F. H. *Appearance and Reality.* 2 ed.; Oxford: Clarendon Press, 1897, chs. XV: "Thought and Reality," and XVI: "Error."

Heidegger, Martin. "On the Essence of Truth," *Existence and Being,* ed. W. Brock. Chicago: Gateway, 1949. The two different views on truth as agreement (*adaequatio*) are drawn from this work.

James, William. *Pragmatism and Four Essays From the Meaning of Truth.* New York: Meridian Books, 1955, Lectures II: "What Pragmatism Means," and VI: "Pragmatism's Conception of Truth."

Locke, John. *An Essay Concerning Human Understanding,* ed. A. C. Fraser, New York: Dover, 1959, Bk. II, ch. 23.

Phelan, G. B. "*Verum sequitur esse Rerum,*" *Mediaeval Studies,* 1 (1939) 11–22. This short but excellent article, "The True Follows the Being of Things," is in English.

Sellars, R. W. "The Correspondence Theory of Truth," *Journal of Philosophy* 38 (1941) 643–654.

3. GOOD

We often use the word "good" in contexts which are principally ethical or religious. Thus we speak of John as a good man, by which we mean that John is a moral person, a fine upstanding individual, a just and kind person. However, we use the word good in a wide variety of other senses which have nothing to do with religion or morals, senses which may even be opposed to these. For example, the criminal may speak of a well-executed bank robbery as a good bank job, although one might not necessarily be willing to grant that it was good in a moral sense.

Many of these nonethical uses of the word good depend to a great extent upon context or point of view. For example, we may speak of the lion as making a good kill when he kills an antelope. It would have to be granted that killing the antelope might be good from the lion's point of view, since it is good for the lion to eat and be satisfied. It may not, however, appear so good from the antelope's point of view. And yet the killing of the antelope taken independently both of the lion's and the antelope's point of view may also be good. For if lions did not reduce the size of antelope herds by killing and eating some, the grasslands would be quickly used up, and all the grazing animals in the plains, and the antelopes as well, would be destroyed.

To take another example: Johnny's parents may speak of having given little Johnny a good spanking, because he refused to eat his vegetables. Johnny's view of the matter may be entirely otherwise: all spankings are bad. Even from the parents' point of view the spanking may be bad, since they do not enjoy it any more than does Johnny. But although spanking Johnny may not make Johnny or his parents feel good, in the long run and in the larger context of Johnny's life as a whole, the spanking may really be the best thing.

There would appear to be good's, better's, and best's in all this, degrees of good according to different contexts and points of view. Thus individual lions are given the grade good, better, or best according to how quickly and expeditiously they can kill an antelope. Similarly the spanking that Johnny receives may be good or better depending upon the effectiveness with which it is administered. It would appear that these degrees of good can be either objective or subjective. The lion may consider a fat, well-fed antelope a much better subject for a kill than one that is thin and scrawny. It is subjectively good. On the other hand, there would appear to be degrees of objective good as well. It is objectively good for lions to eat antelopes to keep the grasslands from being over-crowded, but it is better if they eat those that are lame or diseased.

a. Good as Desired

What, then, does it mean to say that something is good? When Johnny's parents say that the vegetables are good for Johnny, they may be thoroughly aware that Johnny does not think them good. To him they do not appear a subjective good; he simply does not desire them. The parents reason, however, that if Johnny realized how good vegetables were for him, he would desire them. For Johnny's parents are convinced that vegetables are objectively good for Johnny, since they contain the vitamins and minerals necessary for Johnny's health and proper growth. They are something desired for Johnny as "good for him." But although they may be so desired by Johnny's parents, this does not necessarily mean that they are, in fact, good for Johnny. It could occur that Johnny's parents are entirely incorrect about the food value of these particular vegetables, or that they are not what Johnny needs at all. Similarly, it is conceivable that Johnny's parents might not allow him certain vegetables which might, in fact, be good for him.

The good, then, is not necessarily what is desired, whether by Johnny or by his parents. Similarly, what is not desired, whether by Johnny or by his parents, may, in fact, be good. What is good and what is desired cannot be identified. By the same token the diabetic with an insatiable love for milk shakes may very much desire "just one more," but it is not necessarily what is good for him. The diabetic may not desire the bother of taking his insulin shots, and yet this is good for him. One cannot, therefore, equate what is desired with what is good. Some things which are desired are not necessarily good; some things that are good are not necessarily desired.

The fact that the good is not necessarily to be equated with the desired, since it does not necessarily depend upon the different contexts or points of view considered, makes the notion of "degrees" of good at least questionable. It is, of course, perfectly true that from a certain point of view or in accordance with a particular standard or criterion it is possible to consider some things as better or worse than others, that is, arrange them in scales of valuation. However, if the existence of each and every thing is its own, and if the All or None Law is correct, then the being of a being cannot be more or less good. It is, and must be, as good as it is, simply because it is, independent of any particular context or point of view, even though this may be the way in which it has to be judged. The being of a being cannot exist more or less, and hence it cannot, by itself, be more or less good; even though it may be so viewed in relation to some other thing or according to some standard or criterion.

b.   Good as Desirable

But if the good is not simply what is desired, then how is it to be understood? To answer this question it will be necessary to consider, at least briefly, the actual structure of desiring. When something is desired, when something is declared good, whether as objectively or subjectively so, that something must exist outside the one that desires it. If what is, in fact, desired is already possessed, it is not desired; it is enjoyed. What is desired must be something which the desirer does not actually have. The antelope is desired by the lion because the lion sees the antelope as something good, but does not yet have the antelope within his clutches. What is desired exists outside the being that desires it, and the desirer can desire it because he sees it as a good he would like to possess.

Does the good add something to being? Clearly in terms of the All or None Law, the lion's eating the antelope adds nothing to the being or existence of the lion. The lion's existence does not get bigger and stronger; the lion does. Something is added to the lion. And it is exactly because the lion is able to add, appropriate, and assimilate the freshly killed antelope to himself that the lion desires the antelope. It is this "able to add" which provides us with an insight into the meaning of the good. The good is not to be identified with the desires, as we have seen; the good is the desir(e)-able, that is, what is able to be desired.

In other words, the structure of desiring indicates something of the meaning of the good. Desiring implies not simply something desired; for what is desired may not necessarily be good for the "a being" that desires it. Desiring implies a desirer plus something *able* to be desired, that is, something desirable, to constitute the actual fact of desiring. Only because there is an antelope outside the lion able to be desired by the lion, the desirer, can there be such a thing as desiring. And it is this "able to be desired" which is meant by the good. Only in this way could the desiring lion be drawn in its desire toward the antelope. The good, then, is being as desirable. This does not mean that the lion somehow desires the being of the antelope; he desires the antelope. But he is able to desire the antelope only because the antelope does, in fact, exist. The antelope is desired only because it is desirable; but it is able to be desired, that is, it is good, only because it actually exists. The lion does not consume the existence or being of the antelope; he eats the antelope. He does not add the being of the antelope to his being; he appropriates and assimilates the antelope, or what was the antelope. However, because of the necessary interdependence between being and a being, because the being of the antelope can be separated from the antelope only by separating him from his existence, in satisfying his desire the lion makes the antelope cease to exist.

c.   The Good and the True

The good is simply being as desirable. This does not mean that there is necessarily anything which, in fact, desires this thing that is able to be desired. But it is this transcendental aspect of being which makes of the good a lure, something which draws beings to other beings. It is the good, one might say, which urges and forces beings forward in the direction of certain aims and goals in the same way that it is oneness, the basis for the self-preservation of integrity, which drives and forces being from behind. One can see this, for example, in the case of truth. Truth is a good for the knowing mind. It is something desirable because of the particular aspect of being that truth represents for a being that knows. And it is because there is an aspect of the good to truth that truth is desired, and draws the knower on in a continual search for it, wherever it may be found. This is also why there is a certain satisfaction received from the acquisition of truth. Like anything that is good, the attainment or possession of truth in a certain area produces satisfaction.

There are, however, significant differences between the true and the good which it might be well to point out, since these differences may help to throw some light on both of these transcendental properties of being. Although truth is a good for a knowing mind, and is therefore something able to be desired, this does not necessarily mean that it is in every case desirable. Sometimes the truth, once it becomes known, is not desired at all. The truth can be painful, and can bode ill. One may recall the search for truth, along with its tragic consequences, for King Oedipus. In a charming line the German poet Hölderlin remarked that perhaps Oedipus had one eye too many (*Der König Oedipus hat ein Auge zuviel vieleicht*). In other words, it is not possible to identify these two transcendental attributes or properties of being. There are some things that are true, but not necessarily good, from one or the other point of view.

There are, however, other significant differences between the true and the good. For example, the good is being as able to be desired; this means, as we have seen, that it is outside the one who actually desires. Such is not the actual case with truth. Because the mind is fundamentally active in the process of knowing, the truth, as that which is known by the mind, may almost be said to be constituted by the knower. On the other hand, the good, as that which is able to be desired, is not in any way constituted by the desirer. In fact, its being desirable depends upon its existing prior to its being desired, and outside of and independent from the desirer. Finally, in the case of the true, a new existence is given to the being that is known; whereas in the case of the good, particularly when what is desired is, in fact, enjoyed, the existence of that which is desired is destroyed. Thus, for example, in order to know the truth about antelopes, it is not necessary to eat them, merely to give them a new mode of existence in the mind. The lion, on the other hand, can achieve the satisfaction of his desire for food only by destroying the existence of what is desired.

d. The Pragmatically Useful and the Good

Popular pragmatism says simply, "If it works, it's good." Such a view of the good can easily be seen as too narrow and restrictive. For example, one can say that the car is good because it works. But can one retain the same meaning of good for a tree, or for another person? Is the tree good, for example, merely because it is useful? Or is the tree useful because it is good? Does one call another a good friend simply because he is useful?

There is one very good reason why the viewpoint of popular pragmatism is too narrow and restrictive in the meaning that it attaches to the good. In the last analysis it is largely man oriented. For example, is the tree good merely because it is useful for man's purposes, in the sense of something that is desired? To say that what is good is pragmatically useful generally means that the good is defined in terms of what is useful for man. It represents a man-oriented, rather than a being-oriented viewpoint, without, in fact, giving a basis for that viewpoint. We can call this the Homocentric Fallacy, the attempt to define what is or is not good in terms of a specifically human bias.

Are there not, for example, things which are good, and yet which are not useful? Indeed, they would have to be good in the sense of being able to be desired before they could, in fact, be desired as pragmatically useful. But are there not beings which are not at present desired by man, which are yet good, that is, able to be so desired? There was a time, for example, when uranium was not particularly useful, and thus was not desired or mined in any great quantity. This did not mean that uranium was not good, that is, that goodness was not a property of its being. The very fact that it later came to be very much desired was possible only because it was, from the first, desirable, that is, good.

There is, however, another characteristic of the pragmatically useful which must be pointed out. What is useful is generally useful for something else, that is, for some other purpose. Uranium became useful because of its role in atomic fission. It was a means to something else. By the same token money is not useful in itself, but because it is useful ("good for") something else, for purchasing other things or for making more money to purchase yet other things, etc. This is why what is useful as a means to something else is desired. One could continue along indefinitely in a line of things that are useful (desired) for other things, and these for yet other things. But in the final analysis, what is desired can be desired only if it is desirable. And this will be true, to some extent, even of those things which upon which the pragmatically useful, even as a means to some other desired end, would ultimately depend.

e. Summary

In considering good as a transcendental property of being we have attempted to prescind, as much as possible, from the ethical or religious meaning of the word. It was noted that good has both an objective and subjective aspect. One thing, however, became clear: it is not possible to identify the good with what is desired. There are things which are desired that are not good; things good that are not desired. This fact tends to throw a very different light upon the question whether one may speak of degrees of good. Through an analysis of the structure of desiring it was found that the good, as something which must be independent of the desirer in order to be desired in desiring, must be the desirable, that which is able to be desired. Only as such might it add to being, and become the basis for that lure which is proffered to various "a beings." Thus one may speak of truth as a good for the mind; but true and good may not be identified: what is true need not necessarily be good. And clearly the enjoyment of the good and satisfaction taken in the knowledge of what is true are very different. Finally, the view of popular pragmatism was briefly considered, and the Homocentric Fallacy laid bare, by showing that the useful is merely what is desired, not necessarily what is desirable. In fact, it is being as desirable (good) which makes it possible for the useful to be desired, as it is, for something else.

bibliography

Bradley, F. H. *Appearance and Reality*. 2 ed.; Oxford: Clarendon Press, 1897, chs. XVII: "Evil" and XXV: "Goodness."

Maritain, Jacques. *Saint Thomas and the Problem of Evil*. Milwaukee: Marquette University Press, 1942.

Moore, G. E. *Ethics*. London: Oxford, 1912, chs. I and II.

———. *Principia Ethica*. London: Cambridge, 1959, ch. III.

Ricœur, Paul. *The Symbolism of Evil*, tr. E. Buchanan, New York: Harper & Row, 1967, pp. 151–157, 347–357.

Salmon, E. G. *The Good in Existential Metaphysics*, Milwaukee: Marquette University Press, 1952.

Siwek, Paul. *The Philosophy of Evil*. New York: Ronald, 1951, pp. 21–35, 54–74.

Weiss, Paul. "Good and Evil," *Review of Metaphysics*, 3 (1950) 81–94.

4. BEAUTY

Beauty is also a transcendental property or attribute of being. Like the other transcendentals, it will throw an important light upon being and its meaning. It is treated after the true and the good because, as we shall see, beauty has aspects similar both to the true and the good. Like the good, for example, beauty may appear to have subjective and objective aspects. For example, a scientist may consider a formula in physics as beautiful, whereas for the ordinary man in the street it is nothing more than a line of mystifying squiggles. Similarly a biologist might consider a cancer beautiful, whereas within the context of a living organism it might most certainly not be so considered. The beauty of a being would seem to be relative to the context in which it is found or studied.

But in spite of the elements of the relative, the subjective, and the contextual, there would appear to be certain objective aspects to beauty as well. For example, one may in no wise consider snakes as beautiful. They frighten us, disliked because they are slimy and ugly. And yet they are apparently beautiful to snake charmers, or, at least, to other snakes. However, they might also be considered beautiful, in a metaphysical sense, simply because they are, that is, if beauty would really be a transcendental property of being. In fact, one might argue that if snakes were not, in fact, able to be seen as beautiful, they could never be so appreciated by those who do consider them beautiful.

But besides the subjective and relative aspects of the beautiful, it may seem that there are various degrees of beauty. In a dog show,

for example, the judges may present a prize for the most beautiful
dog in each class. In such adjudications the judges do not, however,
depend merely upon their subjective feelings in the matter. Rather,
they attempt to establish certain objective criteria whereby one dog
may be judged as more beautiful than another. In other words, degrees of beauty could be established only upon objective grounds,
which would indicate that beauty and its appreciation does not have
a merely subjective basis. My liking something does not necessarily
mean that it is beautiful. Similarly, my not liking something does not
necessarily mean that it is not beautiful. There are very good metaphysical reasons for this fact, lying, as we shall see, in the relation
between beauty and the true and the good.

a. Beauty and the Good

Beauty is like the good in that just as our desire is drawn to that
which is desirable, so we are attracted by that which is beautiful. In
fact, the element of beauty can be the reason why, in many cases, we
are attracted by something good in the first place. But we are never
fully able to possess the beautiful, in the way that we are sometimes
able to possess what is good. One may consider a sunset beautiful.
The satisfaction gained from viewing the beautiful sunset is not like
the satisfaction gained from eating a good meal. We cannot assimilate a beautiful object the way we can assimilate nourishment into
the organism. We eat steaks; we do not eat paintings, no matter how
delectable they may look. A Cezanne still life may look almost good
enough to eat, but at today's art prices no one would think of eating
it. We do, of course, speak of "feasting our eyes" upon the beautiful
painting, but this is to our "heart's," not to our stomach's, content.

Beauty is also like the good in that it is not simply what is useful.
The useful, as we have seen, is what is desired primarily for the sake
of something else. But something can be desirable, that is, good,
without actually being desired, hence in no way considered useful.
We do, of course, speak of the "useful" arts. However, art is not
simply the useful, even in what are sometimes called the useful arts.
In fact, art adds something over and above the purely utilitarian. The
patterned, and sometimes colored, design drawn on an ordinary cup
or pot as turned off the wheel of the potter, and then fired in a kiln,
do not add to, nor do they take away from the usefulness of the cup

for drinking or the pot for carrying water. They add something over and above mere utility; they add art, and can add beauty. The cup or pot, both by reason of its pleasing shape and the added decoration and ornament becomes a work of art, desired as much for its beauty as for its usefulness as something to drink from or hold liquids. Nevertheless, the beauty of the cup or pot is something we "take in" in a very different way than we take in what the cup or pot contains. "Taking in" a good play is very different from the intake of food. And what makes the difference is the truth aspect of beauty.

b. Beauty and Truth

In his *Ode to a Grecian Urn* Keats wrote, "Beauty is Truth, and truth beauty;—that is all/Ye know on earth, and all ye need to know." The fact that it is a poet, a maker of beautiful things, who should suggest an identification of truth with beauty opens an old philosophical wound. Does beauty, for example, tell the truth? The poet (in lines of poetic beauty) says that it does. But if beauty does not necessarily tell the truth, then perhaps even this statement about the identity of truth and beauty may be more beautiful than true, since it is, in fact, expressed by a poet.

In Book X of the *Republic*, one may recall, Plato had serious doubts about the truthfulness of poets; and this is why Plato would exclude the poet from his ideal state, or at least strongly curtail his activity and censor his products. According to Plato's theory of ideas, the sensible things that exist, the trees, the beds, etc., are each one fashioned or patterned after an eternal and immutable idea of that thing; and it is this Idea that is "truly real." The sensible thing is thereby merely an imitation or copy of that true Idea of Tree or Bed. Now when the artist paints a picture of that sensible bed or when the poet makes verses about the tree, both of which are models for the artist or the poet, the painted picture or the word picture of the sensible, physical object painted represents, in Plato's view, an imitation or copy of an imitation. If the tree which is seen with the senses is but a pale reflection or limitation of the true and perfect Idea of the thing, then the artistic imitation of it represents an imitation of an imitation, and is thus at least two stages removed from true reality. This is why Plato can consider the poets liars.

One may, of course, view the matter otherwise. It may be true to say that the work of art is not a direct copy of what it represents. However, if this was all the painter intended, he might be better advised to seek out a photographer to take a picture of whatever he was painting. In other words, it may be true that the artist does not succeed in making a perfect representation of the sensible object or model before him; but this need not necessarily be understood as his intention in the first place. And the fact that the artist fails to make a perfect representation of the object before him does not necessarily mean that he is a bad artist or that he does not express the truth. Perhaps the artist succeeds in breaking through the mere appearances of sensible things, as mere imitations of the idea, to the idea beyond, and thus to the inner core of reality itself. Perhaps, the artist is not a liar at all, but the one who really tells the truth. And he expresses this truth in the form of beauty.

It would seem, then, that it is not possible to identify truth and beauty, as, in a moment of poetic exuberance, Keats does. There are some things that are true, as Oedipus discovered, which are not necessarily beautiful; and there are things which are beautiful, for example Keats' couplet, which, it becomes clear, are not necessarily true. Beauty can be used as an attractive camouflage or disguise for what is, in fact, not true. Beauty can be used to tell a lie, as Plato well knew. A speech or a book can be beautifully and artistically contrived with either the intention or the result of leading others astray. Beauty can be used to sell a product which the public neither wants nor needs; it can be used as an instrument of propaganda in the machinery of political control.

But although beauty cannot be identified with truth, this does not mean that they are totally unrelated. They would necessarily be related, if only because they are both transcendental properties of being. But as was indicated above, there is an element of truth to beauty. And it is because of this element of truth that beauty cannot be identified with the good. The reason why we do not "take in" an art show the way we take in food is because of the truth element in beauty. In the case of the good we receive the satisfaction of possessing what is desired as good. It is desirable; that is why we are attracted to it. It is because of the truth aspect of beauty that we need not actually possess the object in question to appreciate it. It is not necessary to own an art gallery to appreciate good art. How could we possibly possess a beautiful sunset? We simply appreciate and contemplate the beautiful sunset. Indeed, its beauty attracts us, but unlike the good of an object we might wish to possess, assimilate to ourselves, or to which we might desire to join ourselves, the object of beauty we leave standing where it is, desiring simply to appreciate it from afar. There is, then, truth to beauty, and it is this truth that we contemplate in the appreciation of the beautiful object. There may be some poets or artists who lie, for one reason or another; but lying is not an occupational hazard peculiar to the realms of art.

Clearly, the "truth" of beauty is not the scientific truth which would make an analytic study of the height, weight, physical and ornamental characteristics of a beautiful Etruscan vase, or count the number of times the poet uses a particular word or construction. All these things may be true of the individual work of art, but such facts are irrelevant so far as the total beauty of the object would be concerned. Nor does the artistic truth of a portrait lie in the exact correspondence between it and the model or subject that is painted. As we have seen above, truth is not primarily the mind's conforming itself to the thing, but the thing's according itself to the mind and its modes of knowing.

c. Nature and Art

There is a difference between the beauty of nature and that of art. As an example, one may take the eyebrow. The eyebrow has a certain functional beauty. It is desirable for keeping the sweat out of the eyes while one is working. But even independent of its purely functional value, the eyebrow has about it an aesthetic element, such that without it the face would lack some of its accustomed beauty. This is why a woman may darken her eyebrows with eyebrow pencil in order to emphasize the line of hair arching above the eye. The beauty of art is not necessarily the same. It tends to emphasize the truth aspect of beauty, rather than the aspect of good. Thus we may consider the eyebrow in a Picasso painting, placed somewhere down the middle of the cheek, beautiful within the context of the painting, whereas on an actual person we would undoubtedly consider it grotesque and ugly. There are certain liberties permitted the artist, certain poetic and artistic licenses, which are not permitted the beauty of nature, because of the nature of truth and the specific sort of truth that is artistic beauty.

One of the reasons for this difference between artistic and natural beauty is the factor of context and the principles according to which that beauty is organized. Natural beauty is already set within a certain context, and ultimately within the context of nature as a whole; it operates in accordance with the principles of organic and inorganic structures. In the organic sphere natural beauty stands related to the various goods and goals which each organism attempts to achieve. The world of art also depends upon context. For example, we would not think of hanging a van Gogh in a junkyard; and it would seem strange to see it hanging all by itself in the middle of a forest. Similarly, the principles of the painting's organization lie primarily in the mind of the artist, in accordance with the particular truth of beauty that he wishes to express. The beauty of various natural objects, on the other hand, lies more within them, and in terms of organic or inorganic structures of organization.

But whether in the beauty of nature or in that of art there will always be something of a relative or subjective aspect to what is actually considered beautiful. Indeed, the mind does not wholly create truth; but a mind is required for its constitution. But although a mind is also required for the creation and appreciation of that peculiar kind of truth that is beauty, beauty cannot be wholly relative or subjective. If this were the case, there could be no art critics. The drama critic in his judgment of a new play cannot simply say "I don't like it"; he must be able to indicate reasons why the drama is not an artistic production, why it is not a work of art. He must appeal to certain objective standards and criteria which he has gained through a lifetime of study and appreciation of different dramas from all periods and genres of the art. If the play is not beautiful, there will be reasons that can be given why it is not; and these reasons cannot merely be relative or subjective, even though this preliminary feeling that "I don't like it" may be the reason why more objective reasons are, in fact, sought.

d.   Being as Beautiful

But if beauty necessarily has aspects both of truth and goodness, so that we might be attracted (good) to contemplate (truth) what is beautiful, then beauty must also be one of the transcendental properties of being, if only as the peculiar and unique combination of the good and the true that it represents. This does not, of course, mean that *a* being is necessarily beautiful. By all the canons of present taste it may be ugly. But it is ugliness, not beauty, that is in the eye of the beholder. One may find a Black Widow spider ugly, but to the male of the species she may appear quite beautiful, though fatally so. A being may be either beautiful or ugly, according to the context or in accordance with one's particular point of view, but we are concerned here with beauty as a transcendental property or attribute of the being of a being, not with the beauty, or lack of beauty, of a being. And on this score it would be necessary to say that the being of a being is, *in every case,* beautiful simply because the "a being" does, in fact, exist. For even though it may not be appreciated for its beauty, it is, nevertheless, *able* to be so appreciated. Thus, I may not appreciate the beauty of a Bach fugue, but with more education in musical forms and structures I may be able in the future so to appreciate it.

Hence, like truth, which is being as knowable, or good, which is being as desirable, beauty is being as appreciable, as able to be appreciated. If a being were not beautiful in its being, that is, if it were not something able to be appreciated as beautiful, then it could not later, for example with more education, come to be so appreciated. This "appreciableness" would have to be independent of any special context or particular point of view, since as a transcendental property of the being of a being, it would be able to be appreciated in any context and from any context and from any point of view. Beauty belongs primarily in and to being. If it did not, we could not appreciate the beauty of a being. This means that if something exists, it is beautiful. It has enough goodness that it can attract us; it has enough truth that it can be contemplated in and for itself. And it is this peculiar combination of being as true and as good which assists us in understanding being as able to be appreciated. We may not, personally, appreciate the beauty of an annoying fly; but there is a beauty attached to the very existence of the fly, and this is why a zoologist might develop a genuine appreciation for the beauty of flies through a study of them.

e. Summary

Beauty is also one of the transcendental properties of being, and like the other transcendentals it throws a helpful light on being by describing it "in other words." Beauty contains aspects both of the true and the good, and may be understood as but the combination of the two. Like the good it has objective and subjective aspects, but it cannot be simply identified with the subjectively desired. It is, like the good, something desirable that we would like to appropriate to ourselves. However, the mode of appropriation cannot be that of complete possession, as in the case of the good, because of the truth or, if one likes, the contemplative aspect of beauty. This truth aspect in art or beauty must be carefully dissociated from the view of Plato, for truth and beauty can no more be identified than beauty and good. What is beautiful need not necessarily be true, or what is true, beautiful. Beauty is a transcendental which cannot be considered wholly independent of context, and there is a difference between natural and artistic beauty on this score. One might, of course, say that the appreciation of natural beauty is more universal than that of artistic beauty. But if one understands the being of a being as in itself beautiful, that is, as able to be appreciated, then even though the particular art object were able to be appreciated by no one, except perhaps the artist, it could still be beautiful, that is, as something *able* to be appreciated.

exercises

1. "Good is what I like." Discuss.
2. Can one speak of degrees of good?
3. Does good add to being?
4. Describe the metaphysical structure of desiring. How does this assist us in understanding the good?
5. What does it mean to say that being is good?
6. Compare the true and the good, perhaps using knowledge as an example.
7. Discuss the statement: "The useful and the good are identical."
8. "What I do not like is ugly." Discuss.
9. How does beauty differ from the good?
10. "Beauty is identical with the true." Can this be held?
11. Why does Plato dislike the poets? Give him a dialectical twist.
12. Discuss the statement: "Beauty equals good plus truth."
13. Compare natural and artistic beauty.
14. Does beauty add to being?

15. "I like (hate) metaphysics because . . ." Complete in twenty-five words or less.

bibliography

Collingwood, R. G. *Outlines of a Philosophy of Art.* London: Oxford, 1925.

Ducasse, C. J. *Art, the Critics, and You.* New York: Liberal Arts, 1955.

Gilson, Etienne. *Painting and Reality.* New York: Meridian Books, 1959, pp. 181–197.

Hook, Sidney (ed.). *Art and Philosophy: A Symposium.* New York: New York University Press, 1966.

Hungerland, I. C. *Poetic Discourse.* Berkeley, Calif.: University of California Press, 1958.

Maritain, Jacques. *Art and Scholasticism,* tr. J. F. Scanlan. New York: Scribner, 1930, pp. 23–38, 161–173.

———. *Creative Intuition in Art and Poetry.* New York: Meridian Books, 1955, especially 122–135; note mainly the aspect of the "ugly."

Plato. *Republic,* Bks. II, III, and X.

Santayana, George. *The Sense of Beauty.* New York: Scribner, 1896, pt. I: "The Nature of Beauty."

Sparshott, F. E. *The Structure of Aesthetics.* Toronto: Toronto University Press, 1963, pp. 59–90.

Thompson, S. M. "Existence, Essence and the Work of Art," *International Philosophical Quarterly,* 3 (1963) 527–536.

APPENDIX I:
PARMENIDES AND HIS POEM

Parmenides was an early Greek or pre-Socratic thinker who flourished about the sixth century B.C. at a place called Elea, a Greek colony on the southwestern coast of the boot of Italy. He is said to have been an associate and follower of one of the Pythagoreans. Of his works we have a poem, preserved for us by Simplicius, written in hexameters—as is Homer and Hesiod (the prologue or introduction is reminiscent in style and tone to the opening lines of Hesiod's *Theogony*)—and in the Doric dialect of his locale. The poem may be readily divided into three parts: 1) a prologue or introductory section, 2) the way of truth, and 3) the way of seeming (way of opinion or way of the mortals).

These are the outward facts about Parmenides and his poem. The importance of this ancient thinker for the subsequent history of Greek philosophy, and especially for metaphysics, cannot be overestimated. He has rightly been called the father of metaphysics; and every Greek philosopher after Parmenides had in some way to come to terms with the uncompromising "logic of being" that he introduced. The purpose here is not to give a detailed analysis of the whole of Parmenides' thought, but primarily those aspects which will make more intelligible the approach to a classical metaphysics taken in the preceding pages. For this purpose it has been thought best to use Parmenides' own words.*

1. The Prologue

1. The horses that draw my chariot have borne me as far ever my

*As translated by Richmond Lattimore in SELECTIONS FROM EARLY GREEK PHILOSOPHERS by Milton C. Nahm. Fourth Edition. Copyright © 1964 by Meredith Publishing Company. Reprinted by permission of Appleton-Century-Crofts.

heart might desire, since they have brought me and set me in the famous way of the goddess, which alone carries through all cities the man who knows. Along this way I was borne; for upon it the wise horses drew me, straining at the chariot, and maidens pointed out the road.

And the axle kindling in the nave gave out a sound like the noise of a pipe—for it was sped by two whirling wheels, one on either side—when the daughters of Helius left the abode of Night and hastened to send me into the daylight, with their hands drawing the veils away from their faces.

There lie the gates of the ways to night and day, and a lintel guards them and threshold of marble; the towering portals are stopped with great doors, and requiting *Dicé* (Justice) holds the keys that fit them.

Yet the maidens beguiling her with soft words shrewdly persuaded her to lift with all speed the fastened bar away from the gates. These as they swung back one after another on the posts rich in bronze, fitted in the sockets and set with nails and clamps, opened a wide space between the doors; and straight through by this way the maidens guided my chariot and horses. And the goddess received me graciously and took my right hand in her hand and addressing me spoke in this wise: O youth, who come to my house companioned by immortal charioteers, with the chariot that has brought you, welcome; for it is no evil lot, but righteousness and justice, that has sent you along this way, far as it is from the trodden path of man. You must learn all, both the untremulous heart of well-rounded truth, and the opinions of morals, in which there is no true belief. Yet it is necessary that you learn these also, how they ought to have judged the things that appeared to them, as you pass through all things.

But do you keep your mind away from this way of inquiry, nor let the habit of long experience force you to direct along it an aimless eye, a shrill ear and tongue; but examine by reason this much-contested refutation that comes from me. Only one way is left to tell of . . .

The first thing that must be noted about the prologue is its mythological cast. It is a preparation for a revelation. Its poetic form was most proper for an inspired message, and had been the form used by all the great educative works of Greek culture. Still, this apocalyptic announcement of a new vision of things does not necessarily imply a mystical or religious experience; though neither does it rule this out. The prologue may be interpreted as no more than a mythological preparation for what is to follow, and what is to follow may not appear to be myth. It is clear, however, that the mythical and the logical cannot be so strictly separated at this stage of Western thought. Among the Pythagoreans, for example—and Parmenides is said to have been an associate and follower of one of the Pythagoreans—there was a mixing of mathematical, scientific, and religious elements in a way that is strange to us. Further, Nietzsche in the last century insisted upon this close connection between *logos* and *mythos* in pre-Socratic philosophy.

Whatever may be the view one takes of the mythological or religious aspect of the prologue, a consideration of the poetic imagery reveals a great deal. A symbolism of light and darkness is very strong: Parmenides takes a trip, assisted by the daughters of the sun, who lead the wise horses from the abode of Night, which is the world of ignorance, to that of the daylight, and thus to the threshold of true knowledge. The one holding the keys to the doors opening onto the truth is *Dicé*. If we follow this word back in earlier Greek thought, we find that both in Anaximander (fr. 1) and in Heraclitus (fr. 80) *Dicé* or justice is cosmological principle whereby the opposites get exchanged—hence, "requiting." Though according to Bowra it may represent an Orphic view: the requiter who rewarded good and punished evil.

At the end of his journey Parmenides meets the goddess, who is in fact unnamed, but who indicates that the revelation he is to receive is a boon not given to ordinary men or mortals, and is indeed far from the road they trod. The goddess announces the content of this revelation: the youth is to learn the truth; but he is also to learn what is false; and finally, he will learn why what is false is so. This establishes Parmenides in his position of fully superior knowledge; he will not merely announce the true, or contradict the false view of the mortals by asserting its opposite; he will be able to explain exactly where the mortals make their mistake, and why. All this would be essential if his position of superior knowledge would be fully established.

2.   The Way of Truth

2. Come now, you must hear what I say and remember it, as I tell you of the only ways of inquiry that can be thought of. One, according to which there is (*that which is*) and it is impossible for it not to be, is the way of Peitho (Persuasion), for it follows Truth; and one is that according to which *it is not* and there is necessity for it not to be; and this I tell

you is a way which is utterly obscure. For you could never learn what is not; this is impossible; nor could you describe it.

3. For the same thing can be thought as can be.

4. Look steadily with the mind upon things afar off as if they were near at hand; for you shall not sever what is from its hold upon what is, since it neither scatters itself throughout the world nor gathers itself together.

5. It is no matter to me whence I take my beginning; for to that point I shall return once more.

After the beauty of the trip sketched in the prologue, the doctrine of the way of truth may come as a splash of cold water. In fr. 2 Parmenides outlines the two roads of inquiry; the one, that it is; the other, that it is not. He simply uses the third person singular of the verb "to be" to designate the first road; and the negative of that very for the second. He immediately indicates certain characteristics of the two roads. The first road, namely that which is (existence, being) cannot not be; that is, it must be. This way persuades because it follows truth. The second road, that which is not (non-being, nonexistence), on the other hand, is not a road at all; in fact, it cannot be. One can learn nothing about this road, nor can it be described; one cannot take, or say much about, a road that is not there.

There is, then, only one way or road which is, and hence, which can be thought (frs. 3 and 6). Everything that is, is inseparable from that which is by all the difference between existence and nonexistence. One might consider that which is (being or existence) as a huge circle containing everything that is, the "well-rounded sphere" he describes in fr. 8. Thus he can say in fr. 5 that no matter where he starts, he always returns to that point. This which is, is within the sphere; and that which is outside the sphere (namely nonexistence) were or existed, then it would also be within the sphere. But it does not exist, and cannot.

There is, then, only one road, namely that which is.

7. For this shall never be proved, that the things that were not are; but do you force back your thought from this way of seeking.

8. There is one way left for us to tell of, that *it is*; many signs in this way point to this, that what *is* is without beginning, indestructible, entire, single, unshakable, endless; neither *has* it been nor *shall* it be, since now *it is*; all alike, single, solid. For what birth could you seek for it? Whence and how could it have grown? I will not let you say or think that it was

from what is not; for it cannot be said or thought that anything is not. What need made it arise at one time rather than another, if it arose out of nothing and grew thence? So it must either be entirely, or not at all.

Nor will the power of faith ever allow that anything grows out of what is not except what is not; wherefore Justice has not loosened the chains to allow it either to take its being or to perish, but ever she holds it. And the decision of the matter rests herein: *either it is or it is not;* and so it is decided, of necessity, to give up one way as inconceivable and unnameable—for it is no true way—and to admit that the other is actual and a true way. How then could that which *is* be about to be? How could it come into being? For if it has come to pass or is about to be, then it is not. So becoming is put out of the question, and destruction is inconceivable. Nor is it divisible, since it is all alike; nor is there more of it in one place and less in another, which would keep it from being continuous; but it is all full of what is. So it is all consistent. For what is is contiguous with what is.

But it lies motionless in the limit of mighty bonds, without beginning and without surcease, since beginning and destruction have been removed far away, and true belief has thrust them aside. Being the same and remaining in the same place it likewise lies within itself and so remains locked in the same position; for *Anangké* (Necessity), being the stronger, holds it in the bonds of its limitation which confine it all about. Hence that which is is not allowed to be infinite; for it is in need of nothing, but if it were infinite it would be in need of everything.

Thinking and the thing for the sake of which we think are the same; for without that which is, in regard to which it is uttered, you will not find yourself able to think; for neither is there nor shall there be anything beyond that which is, since Destiny has bound it so that it is whole and motionless; and thus these are only names that mortals have made thinking them to be true: creation and destruction, being and not being, change of place and alteration of shining color.

So, since there is a limit to its extremity, it is finite on all sides, like the bulk of a well-rounded sphere, equally balanced from the center in every direction; for there is no need for it to be greater or smaller in one place than another; for there is nothing that is not, which could prevent its coming together, nor is it possible for what is to be greater or less in any place than what is, since it is all inviolate; for (the center) which is equidistant from every side, is just as much within the limits.

There are various signposts that mark this road. Being, or what is, is without beginning and is indestructible. Were it to have a beginning it would have to come from that which is not; if it had an end it should have to pass into that which is not. Since what is not (nonexistence) does not, by definition, exist, that which is could not arise from it or pass into it. Likewise, being or that which is, is one, entire, all alike, single, solid, indivisible, and continuous. The only "thing" that could divide that which is would be something other than what is. The only "thing" other than being or that which is, is non-being, which is not. Hence, being or existence must be one and indivisible, solid, all alike, and continuous, since it is all full of what is, and contiguous to what is.

Furthermore, what is cannot change or move. It cannot, as a whole, move or change into what is not. But neither could change or motion occur within the sphere of what is; for that would presuppose that there were "gaps" within what is, into which it might move or change. But since such "spaces" could only be other than what is, that is, what is not—and there is no what is not—there cannot be motion or change.

Since there is no beginning or end, no motion or change, there can be no time to what is, that is, if by time we wish to include a past and a future to what is. What is no longer (the past) simply is not; it does not exist. What is not yet (the future) does not exist either. Being or what is has not been nor shall it be, since it is now. That is all there is to what is, namely what is now. Indeed, the mind can consider the past and the future, "looking steadily with the mind upon things afar off as if they were near at hand" (fr. 4) but the mind does this in the now of that which is.

Finally, that which is, being or existence, is finite. Justice (*Dicé*) has not loosened the chains that held it fast; what is, is held within the limit of mighty bonds, locked in position by a necessity which holds and confines it all about by the bonds of a limitation which arise from being itself. There is literally nothing that could prevent its coming or staying together, since only something other than itself (for example, what is not, as that which does not exist) could make it become greater or smaller. Hence, it is and must be finite, since it needs nothing. Were it to need something, that is something which it did not have or was not already, there would be something other than that which is. But there is literally nothing other than what is, hence, Parmenides reasons, being must be finite and complete. It lacks or needs nothing. Were it infinite, on the other hand, it would be in need of everything.

3. The Way of Seeming

Hereupon I cease to give you the veritable account and thought concerning truth; hereafter learn the opinions of mortals, following the beguiling order of my words. For they have settled in their minds to name two forms, one of which they should not name; and therein they go astray. They have set them apart as antithetical in shape and given them special marks that they do not share with each other; to one the airy blaze of flame, which is mild and very light and everywhere the same as itself, but not the same as the other; which is in turn the very opposite of it, flameless night, close and heavy of make. Of these I tell you in the apparent order, so that no mind of mortal may ever surpass you.

6. It must be that that, which may be spoken of and thought of, is what *is;* for it is possible for it to be, but it is impossible for nothing to be. This I bid you think on. I restrain you from that first way of seeking, and also from this one, which mortals, knowing nothing and torn two ways, fabricate; for helplessness residing in their hearts controls the errant thought, and they are carried about like men deaf and blind, all amazed, herds without discrimination, by whom to be and not be are thought the same and not the same, and the way of all things turns back against itself.

And then there is the way of seeming, that is, the opinions of the mortals. The goddess was to reveal to Parmenides not only what is true, but also what is false, and why it is thus, "so that no mind of mortal may ever surpass you." What is it that seems true to the mortals? The very opposite of the signposts or the way or road of truth. The way of truth reveals that what is, is without beginning, without end; it is indivisible, motionless, etc. To the mortals' way of seeming what is has a beginning, has an end, is divided, and moves. Where, then, do the mortals go astray? As Parmenides says, they name two forms, one of which should not be named. They are correct in naming that which is. But in order to have division, motion, beginning, and end there must be "something" other than being which would divide from itself, something other than being into which it might move, something from which and into which being might pass in order to have beginning and end. In other words, the mortals must name the form non-being; they must, in effect, say what is not is.

One should not, of course, be too hard on the mortals. After all, this *is* the way things seem; further, the mortals are at least half right. They do name one of the two forms. And this is exactly why the mortals' way of opinion is a way of seeming. Indeed, it does seem true. Unfortunately, what is only half true is also half false; and in such a twilight world it may not always be possible to differentiate between the two. This is why Parmenides speaks of the mortals as torn two ways. They fabricate a world of confusion in which to be and not to be are thought the same and not the same, each turning back into the other.

4. The Significance of Parmenides

It is difficult to overemphasize the importance of Parmenides for subsequent philosophy. He was, indeed, the father of metaphysics, and the debt to Parmenides' thought should be obvious in the preceding pages. After Parmenides every Greek philosopher had to come to terms, in one way or another, with his powerful and seminal thought: the Pythagoreans, the Atomists, the Sophists, Plato, Aristotle, etc. The problems of motion and change, the one and the many, the finite and the infinite, sense and intellectual knowledge, all of these basic philosophical issues are given a specific direction and greater urgency as a result of the sharp and uncompromising logic of being which Parmenides had introduced. Each and every metaphysics begins, or else is forced to return, to the point at which Parmenides started. "It is no matter to me whence I take my beginning; for to that point I shall return once more" (fr. 5). And so does every metaphysician. This is why Parmenides represents the basic approach to any classical metaphysics; he *is* that classic metaphysics. One may not like the alternatives he has offered, but, for good or ill, he set the tradition and framework within which solutions would have to be worked out. And even those who would attempt to break with that tradition can do so only by returning to Parmenides, and attempting to find other alternatives. And even this can be done only with the assistance of the thought framework which he introduced or the ones which were set up in order to counter his. To react against a tradition once it has been set is not to escape it; for the meaning of that reaction always stands in relation to that original tradition. Parmenides' thought about "that which is" still makes its presence felt. Rather than an *ad libidum* appendix, he is the necessary introduction. Rather than a metaphysical afterthought, he is its forethought.

bibliography

Bowra, C. M. "The Poem of Parmenides," *Classical Philology* 32 (1937) 97–112. A careful analysis of possible sources and parallels for the prologue to Parmenides' poem.

Burnet, John. *Early Greek Philosophy*. New York: Meridian Books, 1957, pp. 169–196. Takes a generally cosmological and materialistic view of the early Greek thinkers.

Cornford, F. M. "Parmenides' Two Ways," *Classical Quarterly*, 27 (1933) 97–111. An important early article.

Coxon, A. H. "The Philosophy of Parmenides," *Classical Quarterly*, 28 (1934) 134–144. An extension of Cornford's article.

Guthrie, W. K. C. *A History of Greek Philosophy*. London: Cambridge, 1965, II, 1–80. A balanced treatment which takes into account everyone except Tarán.

Heidegger, Martin. *An Introduction to Metaphysics*, tr. Ralph Manheim. New Haven, Conn.: Yale, 1959, pp. 110 ff. Contains Heidegger's provocative analysis of Parmenides' fr. 3, also available in paperback.

Jaeger, Werner. *The Theology of the Early Greek Philosophers*, Oxford: Clarendon Press, 1947, pp. 90–108. Identifies a "theological" aspect in the logical rejection of dualism.

Kirk, G. S., and J. E. Raven. *The Presocratic Philosophers: A Critical History with a Selection of Texts*. London: Cambridge, 1957, pp. 263–285. Greek text, translation, and brief but helpful commentary.

Long, A. A. "The Principles of Parmenides' Cosmology," *Phronesis*, 8 (1963) 90–107. A more recent review of the view of the mortals.

Minar, E. L. "Parmenides and the World of Seeming," *American Journal of Philology*, 70 (1949) 41–55. Argues that the world of seeming is not a real world, but a real way of looking at the world.

Owen, G. E. L. "Eleatic Questions," *Classical Quarterly*, 10 (1960) 84–101. Tones down the cosmological aspect.

Owens, Joseph. *A History of Ancient Western Philosophy*. New York: Appleton-Century-Crofts, 1959, pp. 56–78. A straightforward account which includes an assessment of the authorities.

Raven, J. E. *Pythagoreans and Eleatics: An Account of the Interaction Between the Two Opposed Schools During the Fifth and Early Fourth Centuries* B.C. Amsterdam: Hakkert, 1966, pp. 20 ff. Indicates the changed views of the Pythagoreans before and after Parmenides and Zeno.

Seidel, G. J. *Martin Heidegger and the Pre-Socratics: An Introduction to*

His Thought. Lincoln, Neb.: University of Nebraska, 1964, pp. 58–86. Considers Heidegger's incursions into Parmenides in the light of the views of classical scholars.

Tarán, Leonardo. *Parmenides: A Text With Translation, Commentary, and Critical Essays*. Princeton, N. J.: Princeton, 1965. A most thorough and judicious review of all the literature, although I find questionable his position that existence for Parmenides is not finite but infinite (pp. 152 ff).

Verdenius, W. J. *Parmenides: Some Comments on His Poem*. Amsterdam: Hakkert, 1964. Unchanged from the 1942 edition.

Woodbury, Leonard. "Parmenides on Names," *Harvard Studies in Classical Philology*, 63 (1958) 145–160. A brief but excellent article on being as the form that thought must take.

APPENDIX II:
SUGGESTED PAPERBACK MATERIAL FOR HISTORICAL BACKGROUND

Anselm, Saint. *Basic Writings: Proslogium, Monologium, Cur Deus Homo,* tr. S. N. Deane. Open Court (P 54).

Aquinas, Thomas. *Concerning Being and Essence,* tr. G. B. Leckie. Appleton-Century-Crofts.

———. *On the Truth of the Catholic Faith (Summa Contra Gentiles).* ed. A. C. Pegis, vol. I. Doubleday Image (D 26).

Aristotle. *Metaphysics,* tr. R. Hope. Ann Arbor Books (AA 42).

Bergson, Henri. *Introduction to Metaphysics,* tr. T. E. Hulme. Liberal Arts (LLA 10).

Berkeley, George. *Treatise Concerning the Principles of Human Knowledge.* Open Court (P 48).

Collingwood, R. G. *Idea of Nature.* Oxford Galaxy (GB 31).

Descartes, René, *Meditations and Selections from the Principles of Philosophy.* Open Court (P 51).

Hartschorne, Charles. *Logic of Perfection and Other Essays in Neoclassical Metaphysics.* Open Court (P 85).

Hegel. Selections, ed. J. Loewenberg. Scribner.

Heidegger, Martin. *Existence and Being,* ed. W. Brock. Regnery Gateway (16061).

———. *Introduction to Metaphysics,* tr. R. Manheim. Doubleday Anchor (A 251).

Kant, Immanuel. *Prolegomena to Any Future Metaphysics,* tr. P. Carus. Open Court (P 53).

Kierkegaard, Søren. *Philosophical Fragments,* tr. D. Swenson. Princeton (91).

Leibnitz, G. W. *Discourse on Metaphysics: Correspondence with Arnauld; Monadology.* Open Court (P 52).

Lovejoy, A. O. *The Great Chain of Being: A Study of the History of an Idea.* Harper Torchbook (TB 1009).

Marcel, Gabriel. *Being and Having.* Harper Torchbook.

Maritain, Jacques. *Art and Scholasticism and the Frontiers of Poetry.* Scribner (SL 96).

———. *Existence and the Existent,* tr. L. Galantiere and G. B. Phelan. Random Vintage (V 324).

Plato and Parmenides: Parmenides' Way of Truth and Plato's Parmenides, tr. F. M. Cornford. Liberal Arts Press (LLA 102).

Plotinus, tr. A. H. Armstrong. Collier Books.

Schelling, F. W. J. *Of Human Freedom,* tr. J. Gutmann. Open Court (P 73).

Scotus, Duns. *Philosophical Writings,* tr. A. Wolter. Liberal Arts Press (LLA 194).

Spinoza: Selections, ed. J. Wild. Scribner.

Index

All or None Law, 56–57, 71–72, 98
Anaximander, 114
Aquinas, Thomas, 23–24, 25, 48, 53
Aristotle, 5–6, 9, 15, 28, 41, 49, 53,
    54, 78, 119
Art, 104–108
Atomic, the, 68, 73–74, 78–79

Bacon, Francis, 85
Beauty, 65–66, 103
   and being, 108–109
   and the good, 104–105
   and the true, 105–106
Being
   as beautiful, 108–109
   as a concept, 19–21, 38
   existence of, 50–53
   as good, 98–99
   indefinability of, 16–17
   knowledge of, 21–24
   for Parmenides, 115–117
   as a "quality," 18–21, 37–39
   questions concerning, 12–17
   as subject of metaphysics, 9–10
   and time, 53–59
   and the true, 85–88
Bergson, Henri, 23, 54, 86
Boethius, 55

Concept, 19–21, 88–91

Darwin, Charles, 54
Descartes, René, 6–7, 22

Education, 91–93
Einstein, Albert, 26
Error, 80–82, 84, 91–93
Essence, 40–42
   existence of, 47–48
   Law of, 44, 45–47
   parallel with blindness, 48–50
   positive and negative sense, 43–45,
     48–49
Eternity, 55
Evolution, 54, 56
Existence. *See also* Being
   existence of, 50–53
   of ideas, 88–91
   Law of, 45–47, 49–50

First philosophy, 5
Flat Earth Society, 81

God, 5, 13, 39–40, 42–45, 65
Good, 65, 96
   and beauty, 104–105
   as desirable, 98–99
   as desired, 97–98
   and the true, 99–100
   as useful, 100–102
Greeks, 6–7, 25, 78

Hegel, Georg, 20–21, 26, 40
Heidegger, Martin, 11, 53, 54
Heraclitus, 67, 70, 76, 114
Homocentric Fallacy, 101

Ideas, existence of, 88–91. *See also*
    Concept
Individuality, 46–47, 74–76
Infinite, 39–40, 42, 43–44, 47, 117
Intuition, 22–23

Kant, Immanuel, 8, 18–20, 22, 38,
    82, 84
Keats, John, 105–106
Knowledge
    of being, 21–24
    speculative and practical, 24–28
    truth and error, 79–88

Language, 8
Laws
    All or None, 56–57, 71–72, 98
    of Essence and Existence, 45–47
Leibniz, Gottfried, 8, 13–14
Limitation, 37, 39, 41–45, 48–50,
    56–57. *See also* Essence
Logic, 16, 18–21

Marx, Karl, 25–26
Mathematics, 26–27, 68–69
Metaphysics, 5–7, 8–9, 21, 27–28, 119

Nature, 6–7, 107–109
Newton, Isaac, 26, 54
Nietzsche, Friedrich, 114
Non-being. *See* Nothing
Nothing, 11, 13–14, 16, 20–21, 23–24,
    39, 44, 48–49, 55, 57, 115

Oedipus, 100, 106
One, 65, 67–68
    and being, 70–73
    the determination of, 73–74
    and individuality, 74–76
    as unit, 68–69
    as unity, 69–70

Ontology, 8

Pantheism, 13, 45
Parmenides, 51, 54, 56, 67, 70, 76,
    92, 112–119
Peirce, C. S., 27
Physics, 6–7, 26, 54, 73–74
Plato, 11–12, 39, 53, 54, 78, 105, 110,
    119
Poetry, 105–106
Pragmatism, 27, 100–102
Pythagoreans, 112, 113, 114, 119

Question and answer approach to
    metaphysics, 11–17

Sartre, Jean-Paul, 23
Schelling, Friedrich, 13
Solipsism, 13, 75

Theology, 5, 6
Time, 15, 53–59, 117
Transcendental, 35, 37–39, 52–53, 55,
    59, 65
Transcendentals, 65–66, 67–109. *See
    also* One; True; Good; Beauty
True, 65, 77–78
    assimilation of, 85–88
    and beauty, 105–107
    and the good, 99–100
    and ideas, 88–91
    and learning, 91–93
    and the real, 78–79
    truth of statements, 79–80

Unity. *See* One
Useful, 24–28, 74, 91, 100–102, 107

Wittgenstein, Ludwig, 8
Wolff, Christian, 8